Frits E. Lawaetz

The Bull of Annaly

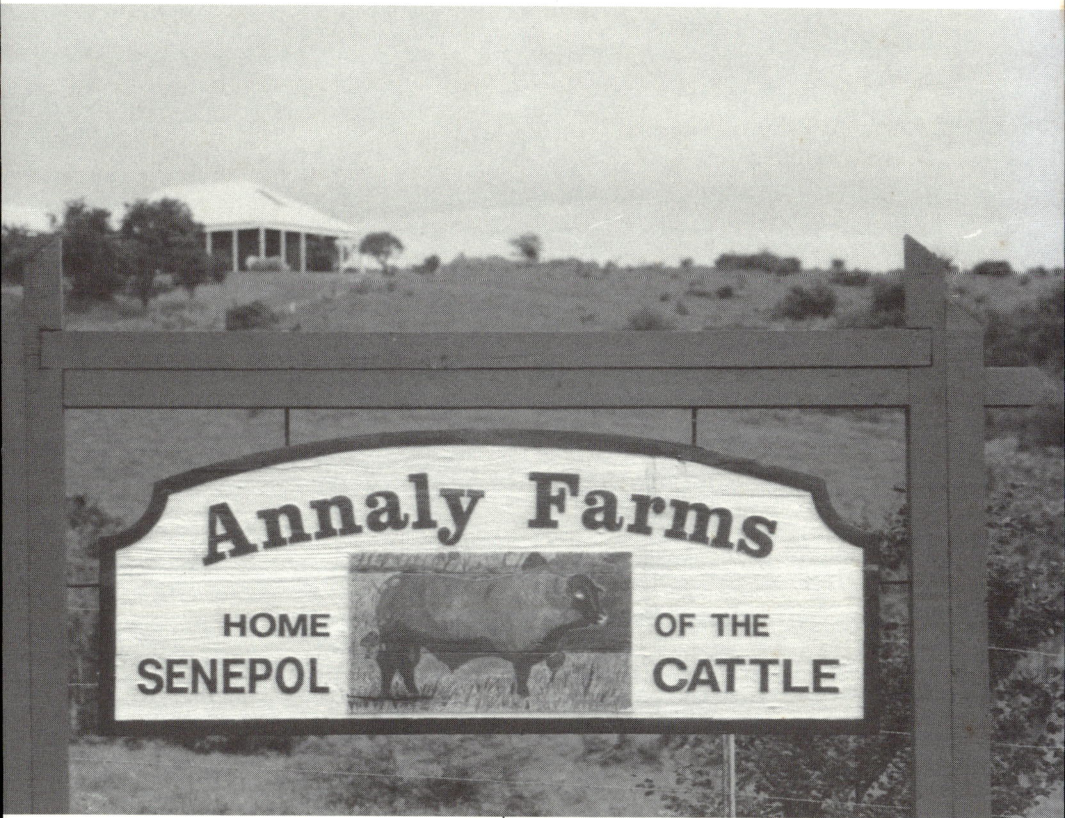

12-13-00

Frits E. Lawaetz
The Bull of Annaly

To:
Mike & Suzanne Masters
Fondly
Frits E. Lawaetz

Priscilla G. Watkins

ISBN 0–9636398–3–8

Front cover photos: Frits Lawaetz in 1976
and Annaly mill and greathouse
Back cover photo: Senepol bull, WC 850

Published by Annaly Farms, Inc.
Box 1576, Frederiksted, St. Croix VI 00841

Composed by Friendly Desktop Publishing
Greensboro, North Carolina

Printed by Thomson–Shore
Dexter, Michigan

Contents

Part III: the Legislative Years

Preface

When Frits first approached me about writing this book in September of 1996, we thought it would take a year, which was all the time both he and I wanted to put to it. Several things interfered, stretching the project out for nearly four years. It took a lot of patience and stamina to remain optimistic, but Frits did, despite the failing health and death of his beloved Bodil; so very special thanks go to Frits for staying the course. This book would not have been as rich without Lawaetz family scrapbooks and farm files. Both Marie and Carl Lawaetz kept detailed records. The extended families also kept photographs and letters, for which I am grateful. The old scholastic method of rote learning helped. I was amazed to hear, on magnetic tapes done ten and fifteen years apart, the same story, word for word, which Frits could tell today without prompting or review. Thanks go to Bob Miller, manager of radio station WSTX in the 1970s and 1980s, who taped Frits's stories on sports. Thanks also to Carol Benedict of Saint Petersburg, Florida, who both taped and video-filmed Frits around 1986, in preparation for writing his biography. She never got it done, although a film script was prepared based on a few incidents. I used her tapes as extra source material. The entire extended Lawaetz family with few exceptions made themselves available for interviews and questions for which I am very grateful. Most Virgin Islanders I spoke with were glad to share their recollections of Frits, the V.I. Legislature, farming, old times and a wide range of other topics during the development of this book. If they don't recognize their version of an event, it is because this book reflects Frits's version of his life, his world and his times.

For assistance with documentation, special thanks must go to Norma Camacho, archivist of the Virgin Islands Legislature, based in St. Croix, for her friendship and cheerful assistance going back to 1977 when I first began to work at the legislature. Norma's memory is prodigious, and she is tireless is searching out ancient records and bills introduced but not enacted. Thanks also to Dr. Aubrey A. Anduze who shared his wonderful memories, as well as loaned us legislative records. Thanks go to Hans Lawaetz who opened up the Annaly Farms records to me, interpreted them, and then corrected my veterinary ignorance or misunderstandings. I learned far more about cattle than I would have ever dreamed possible. Finally, I give most sincere thanks and appreciation to Robert Vaughn, Ph.D., an author, an historian, and good friend, who did the final context editing for me in super–speed time. Notwithstanding all able assistance, any errors or omissions are the responsibility of Frits or myself.

Priscilla G. Watkins

PART I
The Formative Years

— Chapter One —

The Heritage

Frits Lawaetz was sure he wanted to be a cattle farmer like his father by the time he was five years old. That conviction never wavered; among cattlemen he will be remembered for his major role in establishing the first true American breed of cattle, the Senepol, now stocking tropical and subtropical farms worldwide. At home in the Virgin Islands he should be remembered for his successful drive to establish fresh water catchments in the territory and keeping the aquifers alive. Yet at the age of forty–seven, he was drawn away from the farm into running for political office by an act of Congress, which took local government away from his small island home and replaced it with a unicameral legislature based on another island. His belief was that government, to be effective locally, had to be accessible locally. He and all of the inhabitants of the American Virgin Islands were about to participate in the fastest changeover of a society ever accomplished without war as a catalyst: the forced end to an agrarian economy in the islands and the installation of heavy industry, tourism and economic disparity in its place. Throughout his lifetime Frits faced health challenges that many people today would find excuse enough to stop working and let others carry on. His emotional and moral strength came from his family and their expectations; those expectations have their origin in nineteenth century Denmark, seventy–three years before he was born.

Frits's paternal grandfather, Friedrich August Lawaetz, was born in 1834 to a large farming family on the island of Sjaelland, Denmark. At the age of fourteen, he began an apprenticeship in farm work and eventually leased a farm at Molstrup. Friedrich encouraged ministers to preach to his workers and often acted as a lay minister himself. At the age of twenty–five, he married another Lutheran devotee, Christine Amalie Petersen, and began a family. After four girls, Christine, Sophie, Marie Charlotte and Hermia, their first son Carl was born 7 March 1865. He was followed by three more boys, Peter, Otto Charles, and last of all, Poul, born in March 1872.

During the summer of 1872, Carl's father became gravely ill, and his doctor advised bathing in sea water. Friedrich and seven year old Carl set off for Raefsnaesgaard, home farm of Friedrich's older brother Otto, located on the Samso Sound. They only got as far as Kallundborg Ladegaard, also owned by his brother Otto, where Friedrich died on 30 September. Carl was left temporarily at Raefsnaesgaard in care of his Uncle Otto and Aunt Catherinca, how long is uncertain. Then Carl's mother died 7 January 1878 at the farm in Molstrup. Most of the Lawaetz and Petersen family members at Amalie's funeral considered taking on eight orphaned children to be a big burden. Christine, then nineteen, asked to be allowed to stay and work at Molstrup. Some godparents said they could handle one or two at the most, but Uncle Otto would not allow the family to be split up. He packed the seven youngest children up and onto the train to Raefsnaesgaard. The last part of the journey was by farm wagon; the tired little band of travelers arrived near midnight. Otto woke Catherinca, saying she needed to get up because he had adopted seven of his brother's children. Occupied as she was with eleven of their own children, she responded with humor, "Well Otto, the only thing I can say is thanks for the great confidence you have in me!" Frits says that response became his family's rallying cry when things seemed too tough to handle.

Eventually Otto and Catherinca had five more of their own children, raising twenty–three children at Raefsnaesgaard. There was plenty of room; the two–story farm house was three hundred feet long, built for housing many farm hands. Catherinca's great sense of humor and self–confidence kept her household running accurately and happily. Otto owned his own land, among the few Danes of his time with a vote. He took this responsibility very seriously and demonstrated it by participating in every debate and meeting, then sharing the reasoning with all of his children. He was an able farmer. Raefsnaes was nearly self–sufficient in milk cattle, pigs, fowl, vegetables and other farm provisions. Otto and his wife gave equal opportunities and choices to all of the children over their education and apprenticeships. Equally, they shared in the farm and house work.

In 1879, Christine who had remained at Molstrup, married her neighbor and Lutheran pastor, a widower named Edward Nyeborg, becoming his second wife and stepmother to little Marie, who was then six years old. Probably the family, including fourteen year old Carl, attended and celebrated this wedding. Later that year Carl would move to live with his uncle and godfather, Pastor Heinrich Lawaetz in Sattrup, where he studied the Bible for six months. He was confirmed by his godfather on Palm Sunday, 21 February 1880 shortly before his fifteenth birthday.

After Easter Carl began his apprenticeship in farming, rotating every six months between crops and livestock and every two years from farm to farm, to get the most experience in the shortest time under a variety of managers and farm conditions. This style of apprenticeship training is still practiced in Denmark today. Carl kept in close touch with his cousin Herman who, just a year older than himself, was a friend and strong influence. Herman went to university to study for a degree in mechanical engineering, intending to work in the United Sugar Factory which his brother, also named Carl, had built. Soon after gaining his degree however, Herman was drawn to study for the ministry. After his ordination Herman was assigned abroad by the Danish government and sailed with his new wife Ingeborg to the Danish West Indies in 1889. At the end of the nineteenth century, masses of Europeans were moving westward to the Americas; the lure was land. Herman wrote often in glowing terms about the fine weather in the Danish West Indies and the possibilities available for a man willing to work hard.

— Chapter Two —

First Generation in the Danish West Indies

Denmark had first entered the move to the West Indies with the occupation of St. Thomas island in 1672 by its Danish West India Company, which was owned by members of the royal family, some of the king's counselors, merchants and ship owners. In 1718 it occupied St. John and in 1733 bought the island of St. Croix from the French. In the era when sugar cane was king, the Danish West Indian colony was a major player. That era of prosperity was long gone by the time Herman and Ingeborg arrived, but the islands were still places of great beauty and bounty, surrounded by warm and gentle seas teeming with fish and breezy skies that were only occasionally stormy.

In St. Croix, with a population of about eighteen thousand people, Herman Lawaetz became pastor of the Lutheran church in Christiansted. This was a position of great honor as well as responsibility. The church, dedicated as the Lord God of Sabboath Church, sat directly west of Government House which had served, from 1774 until 1871, as the seat of government for the Danish West Indies. The Lutheran church was the official church of Denmark, thus Herman's duties included presiding over all ceremonies of state on St. Croix. He had a comfortable living despite the hard economic climate. Herman and his wife moved into the large parsonage across from the church on King Street, and he began serving as headmaster of the Danish Boys High School, located in Richmond greathouse, a half mile west of the parsonage. He founded and edited the Danish West Indies newspaper and became a member of the thirteen–man colonial council as well.

Herman wrote Carl about the great opportunities available, as the government was selling off foreclosed farm properties. He recommended Carl to the Danish government as a possible manager of crown properties, and a tentative offer was extended. Carl, age twenty–five, was determined to try his luck in St. Croix.

On 23 November 1890, Carl sailed from Copenhagen on the Schooner *Thea*, traveling for forty–two days during the roughest of weather in the northern seas. Herman personally went on board to greet him when *Thea* arrived in Christiansted on 6 January 1891. After a few days of rest at the parsonage, Carl and Herman went by carriage to Sion Farm for a meeting with the government manager, Julius Arendrup. Easily passing muster, Carl began work the following Sunday, as the assistant overseer at $13.33 a month, roughly fifty cents a day.

Sion Farm and Peter's Rest, adjacent estates on a slight hill just west of Christiansted, were run jointly. They had 450 acres in sugar cane, but no mill work was done there. Cut canes were delivered to the central factory near Christiansted. There were forty–eight estate houses with a total of 108 rooms for the one hundred estate workers. Each family had its own garden plot and a little pen or stable for a horse, donkey, goats or pigs. With one hundred people in the village, evenings were both lively and noisy. Archival records for this time period show that the field workers earned between eight and twenty–five cents a day, while carpenters, masons, cartmen and drivers could command thirty to forty cents per day. The average daily pay for a worker was seventeen cents a day, or $4.42 a month. Workers on these estates received free health care and medicine. On Christmas Eve of 1891 Carl was promoted to be head overseer for $16 per month and moved to the big house at Peters Rest. It was here he bought his first "very own nice bed."

A worldwide depression was in effect between 1893 and 1897, depressing markets in the United States of America that had a direct and negative impact on sugar plantations in St. Croix. Long lists of forced sales for debt were posted in the *Avis* newspaper. Rumors were rampant about the possible sale of the islands to the USA, stifling both government and private investment when old George Nelthropp of Estate Boetzberg died. Nelthropp's widow asked Carl to take over some of the plantations as her manager. Carl welcomed the offer, because it meant he could stay even if the islands were sold. On 1 July 1894 Carl became manager of Granard and Cane Garden estates for $25 per month. Money and the opportunity to stay weren't the only motivations; the estates raised cattle, which Carl preferred. There were 215 acres in cane and 940 acres all told. Happy with his cattle work and glad for warm weather in which to work, Carl also began to look for property to buy for himself at auction or at bargain prices.

Both to conserve funds and for the pleasure of their company, Carl gratefully took his meals with Herman and his family at the parsonage in Christiansted. Used to living in a large household, it is likely Carl was an active participant in the lively evening discussions at Herman's tea house. The pastor also ran a community theater group. Certainly when Denmark's Prince Carl came to the islands on a formal state visit, Carl Lawaetz must have attended some of the dinners and balls held in the prince's honor throughout January 1896.

In the spring of 1896, Julius Arendrup, Carl's first employer, contacted Carl about some possible property, and a meeting was arranged. A Mr. Jorgensen of St. Thomas had purchased two St. Croix estates, Little La Grange and Jolly Hill, at auction in 1895 and accepted the experimental planting of pineapples organized by the government's agricultural station at Anna's Hope. He hired the former owner to run the estates, but that turned out to be a mistake, for he did a poor job. Jorgensen was in St. Croix inspecting his estates and, unhappy with his manager, determined to sell them off. Carl impressed Jorgensen as able and responsible so Jorgenson made an offer. The terms were irresistible: two estates, 450 acres, for $12,000 with $2,000 due the first year and $1,000 annually thereafter. Carl agreed to buy them, sight unseen. Carl wrote, years later in Frits's baby book, "On the 7th of April 1896, I bought Little La Grange and Jolly Hill. I moved down from Granard on April 9th and on April 11, 1896, took over full operation of Little La Grange."

— Chapter Three —

Good Management and Frugal Living

At the age of thirty–one, Carl was finally his own boss. The estates, in sugar cane and fruit, were not in good shape in April 1896. But by the end of 1898, they were showing the effect of good management and frugal living; his income was enough to cover expenses and still have some to save. His Jolly Hill house with five horse stables was rented for $10 per month, he made $80 monthly in wood sales, $100 monthly in milk sales, $120 each month in grass feed sales, plus, from time to time, he had income from the sale of fruits, pigs and cane. Carl had repaired all of the estate's village roofs by December 1898; only the greathouse at Little La Grange was still in shingles, but it was sound. The village houses also had new windows and doors, and floors and walls were repaired. Eighteen rooms in the village were rented, as was the overseer's house with its three apartments. Carl, living in his two–story greathouse, was ready for a wife.

The following year created a hardship though. On 8 August 1899 a major hurricane ripped through the island, tearing the roof away from Carl's house and destroying his sugar processing factory. Unable to get financing for repairs, he dipped into savings to pay for new galvanized steel sheeting for the greathouse roof. The factory roof was never replaced; over the next few years Carl hauled his sugar cane stalks by cart to Sprat Hall for grinding. A year later

Carl's estates were valued at $16,000, although he wrote he would take no less than $24,000 for them — double his purchase price of four years earlier!

By June 1901 Carl had paid off half of his mortgage, but he had not yet found a wife in the Danish West Indies. Whether it was a lack of eligible Lutheran ladies, or his apparent dedication to hard work leaving little time to pay court, when Carl went to Denmark to see his family in 1901–02, he was still looking.

He found and proposed to a highly educated, well traveled, unmarried teacher named Marie Nyeborg. The Lawaetz and Nyeborg families had long been neighbors. Marie was born on 7 March 1873 near Soro, sharing the same birth date as Carl, who was born eight years earlier. Marie's mother died when she was six months old. Carl's eldest sister Christine had married Pastor Edward Nyeborg and become Marie's stepmother in 1879. Although Christine died around 1880–81, soon after giving birth to her only child Johannes, the pastor's third marriage to the children's tutor gave Marie and Johannes additional siblings: Asta, Paul, Aage, Hannah, Mia, Titter and Eddy. Marie's father would serve as pastor at Stenmagle for thirty years, commencing in 1885. This church was near the Lawaetz farms, and it is likely Marie met Carl many times before he moved to the West Indies.

Marie and Carl became engaged in Copenhagen on 17 January 1902; she began to plan for an August departure to the Danish West Indies. Shortly after their engagement, the United States president signed a treaty to purchase the Danish islands for $5 million; the U.S. Senate ratified the treaty on 19 February. The possibility of the transfer did not deter Marie. Carl sent money for her passage to St. Croix. In August her father traveled as far as Hamburg with Marie where she boarded the German Ship *Canadia*; he gave her money for return passage, just in case she changed her mind.

On 30 September 1902 at noon, Marie, twenty–nine, married Carl, thirty–seven, in a ceremony led by his cousin Herman at Lord God of Sabboath Church. Carl's good friend and tenant at Jolly Hill, Pastor Niels P. Nygaard, gave Marie away; best man was

Oberst Loejnant Rambusch. "Herman and Ingeborg kept the luncheon" for them, and later that afternoon they drove by horse and carriage to Little La Grange. On 22 October they learned that the Danish senate had rejected the sale of the islands by one vote, that of a ninety–one year old man who was brought into the chamber in his wheelchair.

Carl and Marie (Nyeborg) Lawaetz were married in 1902. They are pictured here in 1908 with their first three children, Anna (l), Else (r), and Frits.

— Chapter Four —

The Second Generation

Marie quickly took over control of her new home. It was a square masonry house with a second story built of wood, hip roofed, settled snugly between three high hills. The front entry faced gently sloping land running west to the sea. There was a long central room used for dining and entertaining with a double door and large window at each end. On the south side was a bed–sitting room at the eastern end and a smaller room to the west. The north side held Carl's farm office looking west and a long service room behind. Typical for its time, the cookhouse was a building of its own outside the northeast corner and just a few steps away from the main house. Carl had purchased a fine set of oak dining furniture, and still had his fine big bed. Marie brought her elegantly made sewing cabinet, a confirmation gift from her father, and painting materials.

With hired staff to do the heavy work of cooking and laundry, Marie spent her free time developing a charming flower garden on the south side of the house and eventually had a summerhouse built there. The garden has acquired many walls and raised beds which surround the house, for Carl loved to build. Stone steps lead to an upper garden built into the hillside.

Marie also supervised the cleaning, cooking and proper preserving of foods. She likely needed a lot of time to direct wash day activities, because both she and Carl favored the wearing of all white clothing in the hot climate. Her intensive training in tailoring, painting and sketching was also put to use. A talented woman, over the years Marie painted many beautiful sets of bone china, sewed fine linens for tables and beds in her own house and for those of her family and friends. Marie became active in Lutheran church work, a natural extension of her outgoing personality. Carl himself was dedicating much time to church work as well. Carl's tenants and friends at Jolly Hill were the Lutheran pastor in Frederiksted, Niels P. Nygaard and his wife, who helped Marie adjust to island ways. It is most probable that Marie joined in petitioning Denmark's Crown Princess Louise to send Lutheran deaconesses to the colony, to provide home nursing services for new mothers.

On 28 January 1904, without such a service, Carl and Marie's first child, Anna, was born. The family held a great celebration for her christening at the Lutheran church. In September of that year, the petitioned deaconesses finally arrived to establish a children's hospital in Frederiksted, and Marie began a lifelong friendship with the Danish missionary women. They were a great comfort to her when the Nygaards transferred to the parsonage in Christiansted early in 1905. Marie was able to use the deaconesses' postpartum service when, in the predawn hours of 27 July 1905, Else, "blue eyed and dark haired and big–nosed," according to her father, was born. While Carl's house was filling with the wails and cooing of infants, his cousin Herman, hard hit by malaria in 1903 and never fully recovered, was preparing to return to Denmark with his family. On the first day of August Carl went up to Christiansted alone to see Herman, Ingeborg and their six island–born children off to Denmark.

Carl and Marie also made plans for a trip to Denmark, to display their babies to the families. The trip by steamship in May 1906 took four weeks. While they were in Denmark, Christian IX, king since 1863, finally died of old age. He was eighty–eight. Carl and Marie likely mourned his death as they would any elderly family member. When Carl and Marie returned to St. Croix in the spring of 1907, their estates were in a neglected and overgrown condition. Carl set to the hard work of reclaiming rough pastures for his 175 head of cattle. Marie, now thirty–four, was pregnant with her third child in five years.

On 5 October 1907, at thirty minutes past midnight, on Saturday, a hefty male child was delivered of Marie in the big bed at Little La Grange by the deaconess midwife, Joanna Sivertsen. Named Frits Eduard, he weighed eight and seven–tenths pounds. "Long of body, short faced, bald, with large blue eyes," the first boy in the household was cause for great rejoicing. Marie, or "Mor," as she became known to everyone, began a baby book in Danish for Frits as she had done for Anna and Else before him.

As Frits's christening day drew near, the house at Little La Grange was burglarized in the night, the first such problem ever for the family, and everyone was questioned. A horseman who suddenly quit a few days earlier was eventually found to be the culprit, but that did not mend hurt feelings. The cook was so insulted at being questioned that two days before Frits's christening she quit. Despite the chaos, Frits's great party went on as scheduled with new hands in the kitchen. Baby Frits was christened in Frederiksted's Lutheran church on 1 December with a full complement of sponsors, including two godfathers living in Denmark, as well as Mrs. Westergaard (the pastor's wife), Miss Joanna Sivertsen and Miss Joanne

Frits, one year old, October 1908

Gautier, missionary sisters.

"Little Brother," as Frits was called, "throve." When he finally got hair on his head, three vortices showed up prompting Dr. Petersen to claim he was going to be a wise boy. Marie did not breast feed this baby for long; he was growing so fast he was placed on the bottle soon after birth. Common to his generation, he spent his first year sharing the big bed with his parents and wore dress–like garments until he began to walk. Like all other babies of his era, he was bathed in sea water. Buckets or casks of sea water were hauled to the house for this purpose. "Teething," Mor wrote, "was difficult for Frits but walking was easy." By early December 1908 he was walking alone and began wearing britches.

Frits spent much of his childhood uncomfortable amid strangers; as a baby, he would hang his head down to the floor in embarrassment, until they were out of sight; as he matured his behavior improved but his reticence did not. In fact, until long after he married, Frits was called the "Silent Dane." Frits became deeply attached to his nana, Dorothea Borea James, who came to the family when he was about six months old. Frits was a studious little infant, "very serious," Mor wrote, "but still active and loud." By the time he was a year old he was wrapped in the daily ritual of morning and evening prayers, and sang from his picture book on Christmas Eve, in mimicry of his parents singing from their hymn books.

Sometime in 1908 or 1909, the cookhouse burned to the ground. A new cookhouse was built and was attached to the northeastern end of the main house. Its east door opened onto a path to the servants' apartment; the south door connected the cookhouse to the service room by Carl's office. It was quite a modern cooking room with griddle pan space built into the top of the firebox. The walls were again painted blue, a color said to repel flies, and baskets and containers hung from the ceiling to hold provisions close to hand but away from wildlife such as mongoose, mice and rats that got in no matter how tightly one closed up. Above the cookhouse Carl created a small room, also attached to the house, which the family called "puttekammer" or the "put anything in" room. Leading up to the new room was a curving stone staircase on the north side, so Nana Dorothea could reach the children more quickly from her apartment. It made it much easier for the family to get to the outhouse, too, with just one door to open. Upstairs off the puttekammer, in typical island fashion, the second floor was almost an exact duplication of the first floor, and the design of one half reflected the other: a large central sitting room flanked by two bedrooms on each side, one large, one small. On the second floor a wide gallery sat above the front porch on the west end, with many windows to provide good working light as well as wonderful views to the sea.

Sister Joanna Sivertsen

For his second birthday, Joanna Sivertsen, one of Frits's godmothers who taught herself photography, came and took photos of all the family. For gifts he received a pull cart and a Danish flag. Because Frits heard the troops and the public shout "Hurrah," when the Dannebrog was raised, he assumed that was its name. Shortly after this birthday he developed whooping cough, "which made him very ill, coughing up blood," Mor wrote. Frits recovered by Christmas and was able for the first time to really participate in the fun of the gifts and dancing around the Christmas tree. Marie's sister and the children's aunt, Asta Nyeborg, arrived from Denmark, bringing a lovely carved wooden stick horse as a gift from her parents, but Frits was very disappointed because the horse had only two feet.

— Chapter Five —

The Cowboy Life

Frits fell in love with the cows and horses before he could walk. He was most happy when his dad, his "Far," took him along in the evening to see the calves in their pen. Those activities were topped only when Far would take him along on walks to the pastures. Theirs was a leisurely stroll, checking for new growths of brush to be rooted out or breaks in the fence line to be mended. In 1901 Carl had begun his first book of careful documentation of birth, parentage, breeding and weights of every calf, cow and bull that lived on his estate. Originally known by numbers, with the arrival of Marie and the children, the cattle were given names and Frits was learning each one. By 1910, Carl's holdings in cattle were so developed the family no longer had to sell wood in Frederiksted but did sell pasture grasses for horses stabled in town.

Frits was moved out of his parents' big bed and into a room of his own at the age of one year. Because of it, Mor recorded in his book that he often moped about; he complained that "nobody loves me." When Frits was a little over two years old, Kai was born on 14 January 1910. Frits loved playing with the baby and would often say "me love Mor and Kai," his melancholy apparently forgotten. His difficulty in speaking continued to cause him much childhood loneliness his Mor said; Nana Dorothea and Else were the ones who understood him best. Frits also had a "best friend" named Joe Bromstaff, the head gardener, who talked while they worked together on the family vegetable gardens.

Carl had the world by the tail, so to speak, with sons to inherit the fruit of his labors and daughters to help their mother. Little La Grange and Jolly Hill were standard cattle raising estates and, like the others, raised their own vegetables, chickens, goats, pigs and guinea hens, with cattle for milk and beef. Carl also grew fruit and cane for sale. Carl's estates earned enough money to pay for a full complement of workmen and keep nana, as well as another servant and cook for his family. They had piped water from their reservoir taking care of all but the drinking and cooking needs of the household.

Carl's primary products were cattle and milk. Careful husbandry and knowledgeable purchases had increased his herd from seven cows which came with the estates in 1896 to nearly two hundred head in 1911. His cattle were mainly N'Dama stock, a gentle African breed from Senegal, hardy and accustomed to hot, humid weather. They also have very long horns and often injure themselves and each other, as well as their handlers. Cattle farms are not cheap to maintain, although they make better use of hilly and dry island conditions than cane ever did. Cattle farms require dipping vats, wells, yards for calves, yards for bulls, yards for ailing cattle and good pasture lands. Given that Little La Grange and Jolly Hill receive an average of forty to forty–five inches of rainfall annually, the Lawaetz family knows, after one hundred years of ranching there, that they need about three acres for each cow. Furthermore, in 1911 it was costing $20 an acre annually to keep the land cleared of water–sucking brush. The islands had a bare look: every hilltop was cleared for pasturage or cane planting; St. Croix and St. Thomas had no forest left at all. St. John was better forested, mainly because it was hard to farm. Carl's hills were carefully planted to the "best grazing" grasses available for the tropics.

Instead of taxes, estate owners under Danish rule were responsible for maintaining roadways along their estates, including access rights of way for foot travelers. Between October and the end of January each year, the government required that owners rake and fill holes on public roadways. Once that was done, the public works department, with help from seasonally idle agricultural workers, laid gravel on all the roads. Carl took advantage of the assignment and had his men rake roadside leaves into large holdings to create mulch for his vegetable beds.

Another member of the family, Otto Charles, Carl's brother, was living in Frederiksted at this time, serving as pharmacist at the apothecary; he was often a visitor to Little La Grange. When Frits was three, Otto Charles gave Frits a wooden horse much loved for its four legs. Frits named it Claus, cut grass feed for it, and each night Claus was put to sleep under Frits's bed. Frits also had an old piece of iron that he treated as if it were a gun; every time he saw a mongoose or a pig he would aim it at them and "fire."

Frits still had great difficulty with speaking clearly; despite encouragement from family, Mor wrote that he spoke mostly English except for nightly prayers. English was just fine as far as the Lawaetz children were concerned. They found their first playmates among the children of Little La Grange village, across the road from home, where everyone spoke English. Dabbling in gut (or stream) water, helping in the provision grounds, chasing dogs, surrounded by dozens of youngsters playing after chores, village life was always active. Frits recalls that his lifelong friendship with Harold, Charley and Arthur Samuels began when they were just babies.

On 30 November 1911 Carl and Marie's fifth child, little Asta, was born. Frits, age four, was just in love with her. Soon after her birth, both Aunt Asta and Mor became drastically ill; Christmas celebrations were limited and baby Asta was not christened until 23 January; Frits was crib–side all through the crisis, constantly tending to "his baby." In the spring of 1912, Mr. Jacobsen of Estate Punch came to manage the estate. On 19 May that year, Carl and Marie left for Denmark once again to spend time with the families. It must have been quite an undertaking with five little children and just Aunt Asta to help: baby Asta was six months old; Kai, two and a third years; Frits, four years and seven months; Else, nearly seven; and Anna, eight and a third years. Several members of the family got seasick. They arrived in Copenhagen on the eleventh of June, with Frits still very shy of strangers and hesitant in speech. Mor wrote that Frits enjoyed going by train to Stenmagle to the Nyeborg homestead. It took him a few days to feel at home, she said, but he finally relaxed with Mor's half–brothers, Paul and Aage. Aage had an old rocking horse he let the boys ride, and Paul took Frits sailing. Frits made best friends with the gardener, Niels, with whom he went everywhere.

The family visited Raefsnaesgaard where Carl and his siblings were raised by Uncle Otto and Aunt Catherinca, enjoying the beach, collecting shells. This trip to the vast farms of Uncle Otto confirmed for Frits that he would be a farmer for sure when he grew up. Back in Stenmagle in October, home to the Nyeborgs, Frits was given a party in the garden for his fifth birthday. He received a pull cart that reminded him of his own at home and a set of blocks that kept him occupied all winter. In November the family moved to Copenhagen, where Frits attended day care at Mrs. Lunding's center, learning crafts and sledding in Frederiksberg park. He particularly liked to go to the zoo and the boardwalk, watching the ships sail by. He recalls a dead, beached whale, kept intact by the freezing weather, where people could walk into the mouth, as if it were a museum piece. Unused to such frigid winter weather, a bad cold infected Frits's lungs by early spring, confining him to bed for three weeks. Mor praised God that Jesus saved his life. Then a fungus infection under his toenail became critical, needing medical attention. His bravery prompted his father to give him a gift of a new book, a special favor he still recalls.

In June the family returned to the parsonage at Stenmagle, and Frits shared a room with Paul. When Paul returned from school each afternoon, the two would happily go out with slingshots to shoot away the birds that ate cherries off the trees. This stay in Denmark was particularly long for the Lawaetz family; why it was so long is not clear. Marie's health may have been seriously fragile. Perhaps Carl wished to study the new centrifuge machinery being installed in Danish dairies. Whatever the reason, after more than a year in Denmark, the family boarded a steamer for St. Croix on 28 July 1913. Frits says he was not as seasick returning as on the outbound voyage, and he and Kai made friends with some of the gendarmes on board. They arrived home on 24 August 1913 after an absence of fifteen months. While they were away the first telephone company had been established on the island of St. Croix in February (St. Thomas had been served since November 1906).

As she had on every big occasion since his birth, Mor entered a summary in Frits's baby book: "The children were so delighted to return the house rang for days with their clatter. The old ties with Joe Bromstaff were renewed and you helped him haul weeds from the garden to the bullpen in the little cart. On your birthday on Sunday the Munters and Tornoe's three girls, Annette, Bodil and Nina, came, as did Miss Sivertsen." Frits was old enough to share out the pieces of cake made in the shape of a man. His gifts were a child sized rake, hoe and spade, tools for the real working world. Every night, as he had done in Denmark, Frits would close up the bars on the crib bed for little "Tulle," his nickname for Asta, and kiss her good night through the cross bars.

Anna, Else, Frits, Kai and Asta, 1913

— CHAPTER SIX —

Home Again

The Lawaetz family resumed their active life in Frederiksted in the fall of 1913. Both Far and Mor were deeply involved with their faith and church. Far had been a founding member of the Blue Cross Society in May 1905 (formerly the Christian Temperance Union), and was a lifelong member of the church council. Mor renewed her work with the Young Women's Christian Association, begun in December 1907 by her two friends, Joanne Gautier and Joanna Sivertsen. Mor made sure all of her children participated in morning and evening prayers, and when they were unable to attend Sunday school, Mor would read stories from the Bible and hold classes at home. Mor was a very accomplished teacher. She first taught her half brothers and sisters for three years at home in Denmark; later she took several courses in Copenhagen and passed the state examination as a teacher in arts. She had taught art in Denmark for three and a half years and Sunday school as well.

The Lawaetz's social life was rich too, although Asta, Marie's sister who had been serving as the children's nanny, had not returned to St. Croix. Otto Charles, Carl's brother, had transferred to the apothecary in Christiansted but came west from time to time. Mor and Far were close friends with the Nordbys of Estate Mt. Pleasant; their sons, Rudolf and Jeffrey, were playmates of Frits and Kai (Rudolf would grow up to become the Queen of Denmark's private physician). Frits made a close friend of Frants Madsen, whose father ran the lighthouse at Ham's Bluff. The Andreasens and Jensens of Estate La Grange, the Nyholms from Estate Envy, and Lindeborgs and Tornoes of Frederiksted added to the pleasure of their days. And the routine of life went on as before.

The milking day starts early. While Far supervised and the other men milked, Frits, who often was the first one up in the mornings, would check the calves for any new little problems. After breakfast and prayers, he would go off to work in the garden with Joe Bromstaff or mount up to check pasture fences with his father. By the time he was six, he was spending his free time from early morning to evening helping with the calves or in the hills, on foot or by donkey, looking for soursop, custard apples, coconuts and mangoes, or guavas at Jolly Hill. For fun, he and the village boys would fish in the guts for shrimps and eels. Although they were forbidden to do so, they also swam in the reservoir above the village as often as they swam in the gut at Jolly Hill or in the sea.

Anna, the eldest, reserved and high strung, chose household tasks over yard work. She preferred cleaning lamp glasses, trimming wicks and sewing to being out in the heated air. Else was known as a "tomboy." She started raising so many chickens she became "Chicken Else." She also raised pigs and goats to sell and enlisted Frits to help her with them. Later Kai was lured into the effort. Fruits were collected for the family table, resale and for Else's pig, Trine. All of the children were crazy about ball games, particularly cricket and, if there were not enough players for a full team, created new rules. In the coolness of the late afternoon, Frits would put Asta in his cart and pull her around.

Little Erik was born on 28 December 1913. One of the stories about births told to children of that era was that newborn babies were brought to the family by an angel, who would leave it on the stair. When Frits came into Mor's bedroom the morning of Erik's birth, he was awestruck and asked Mor if by chance she had seen the angel. Frits's love of babies was well grounded by then, and he was delighted to have another to love as he loved his little "Tulle." Yet, while his infant days were full of pleasure and work, Frits still craved to go to school.

Frits often rode along when Anna and Else were taken to school in the cart pulled by the brisk and efficient little mare called Queen Mary. Evidently he felt left out; the previous winter he had gone to the play school in Copenhagen, Miss Lunding's day care, where his mother had taught art, and he agitated to attend school in St. Croix. Finally, on 14 April 1914, Frits started school and "Far had to do without his little assistant manager." His godmother Joanna Sivertsen gave him his first ABC book and pencils; his teacher was Mrs. DeCastro. He was so eager to learn that the alphabet was conquered within a month's time. Every morning and evening as he changed his clothes, he demanded Far test him with calculations. Highly competitive in school, at the end of Frits's first year he ranked number one and won a picture book as the prize. Mor entered into his book that "he was very proud."

Anna with horse and cart that took the children to school

— Chapter Seven —

Learning about Life

With academic success and his first months of real school behind him, Frits's summer of 1914 was perfect. Once he completed his chores of collecting feed for Else's chickens and testing her hens for eggs by inserting a finger in the hens' rectums, he would gather grass for her goats and his own wooden horse as well. When he could, Frits would walk with Far to check pasture fences for breaks, or go hiking with Anna and Else, scouring the hillsides for ripe fruits. Most days Kai and Frits would put baby Erik and little Asta in the pull cart for rides around the flat lawn before the house. He helped Joe Bromstaff, who had elephantiasis in his right leg, in the kitchen gardens using his own child–sized tools. If his parents were shocked by the assassination of the Austrian heir and his wife on 28 June, or by Austria's declaration of war against Serbia a month later, no word about it was allowed into his baby book.

Towards the end of summer, when he was nearly seven years old, Frits got a bad cut on his leg. An infection in the cut caused a major fever which forced the child into bed. Frits had to remain there for some time after the fever receded, because the cut didn't heal properly. Throughout his slow recovery, he spent time reading fairy tales written by Hans Christian Andersen and telling Bible stories to whomever he could capture to listen. His mother noted that he had a great number of cuts and bruises as he tumbled through boyhood, but this may have been the injury which, later in life, cost him his leg.

Despite the hazardous world of contagious diseases and large livestock in which he lived, he was fortunate to avoid serious health problems as a child. Besides the normal bumps and bangs, often self imposed by dangerous feats, he survived whooping cough at the age of two, had chicken pox when he was ten and a half, and got dengue fever the month he turned fourteen. Frits remembers having chiggers imbedded in between his toes and having to have them dug out — both painful experiences. He had a few tooth troubles, but the only recurring problems were with his eyes which needed drops, probably due to dust.

So the last days of summer were quiet for Frits. On his seventh birthday his mother allowed him to look at his birthday table before class. Frits was delighted to spot a new cricket bat and soccer ball. In the afternoon his godmother, Miss Sivertsen, brought him a large Danish flag and a beautiful set of horse reins. Mor invited his school friends, Harvey and Volmer Larsen, Frants Madsen and Ralph Skeoch, for a party. The gifts of a cricket bat and his wonderful new reins defined a new segment of his life independent of the family circle. The reins gave him tighter control over his donkey Violet, and he was able to travel much farther from home. Cricket and all sports became a passion. The west lawn rang every afternoon with the shouts of the village and Lawaetz children at play, and every afternoon Mor would bring out fruit drinks and sandwiches to force a temporary rest period on their sweaty little bodies. Autumn raced by in a blur of school days, ball games and household chores.

Christmas again was traditional: the family had a small ink-berry tree set up by the stairs in the dining room. It was decorated with little paper Danish flags, cornucopias of sweets, and tiny thin candles. Older members of the family went to the 5:00 P.M. Danish service in their phaeton on Christmas Eve. After church it was the time to open presents. One splendid gift that year was a big pull cart for Frits and Kai, specially made by a carpenter, but the wheels proved fragile and later Far replaced them with old machine wheels. On Christmas the entire family attended the Lutheran service. On

Christmas second day it was Carl Lawaetz's custom to share the meat of a bull with all of the residents of Little La Grange village and to have a party on the front lawn with dancing, something Frits enjoyed with gusto. They sang carols and everyone got presents again. Erik's first birthday was quietly marked.

For much of January Frits was in limbo with a bad boil under his foot. The treatment finally, which relieved the condition, meant putting his foot in near boiling water, then having the core twisted out manually by his nana. Although he had begun work in his third grade infant reader, he felt better when his mother read to him. He recovered in time to join Anna's eleventh birthday party on 28 January. On 4 February little Asta became sick with a throat infection. Bacterial infections were now understood; specific identifications began thirty years before. Although the doctors knew to call her condition diphtheria, the knowledge did not matter because effective treatment was not available in the islands. The infection slowly spread to little Asta's kidneys, making her skin leathery to touch. It formed false membranes across the air passages in her lungs and she labored to breathe. Finally it stopped her heart. Frits's beloved sister was just three and a half years old. Carl and Marie's mountain of faith in God and daily prayers were a great support during those difficult days of watching Asta's life slipping away. Marie wrote in Frits's baby book, "On Sunday, February 21, 1915, God took our little Asta home to himself. Shortly after she died, all you children came up and saw her. We sang the beautiful hymn 'I Know a Beautiful Garden' that she so often sang with us...."

For her funeral, Asta was clad in a white dress and laid out in the parlor; white roses were laid on her chest. Frits thought she looked like a little angel. The following day, before the official service, Mor had little Asta's coffin moved over to their summerhouse in the garden where she had played so often. Here the family sang "We See the Big White Throng." Far thanked God for the time the family had Asta, and they all said a prayer for Asta. In the church, Mor wrote, everyone sang her favorite bedtime song, "The

Bells are Ringing." At 4:00 P.M. Asta was buried in the Frederiksted cemetery. All her brothers and sisters watched carefully. Frits has never gotten over the loss of Asta; it was a profound sorrow for this seven year old child. Although he accepted it and prayed for a long time that she would be happy up there, the memory of that loss has lasted all the days of his life.

That Marie suffered too is evident in her writing. She said Frits was brought home by Mr. Blackwood of Annaly after his classes for the rest of the term. He and Ralph Skeoch, an orphaned grandson being raised by the Blackwoods, would compete vigorously for first place in all their shared grades. This year Ralph came in first. Frits was inconsolable for days after he learned that his teacher for the past eighteen months, Mrs. DeCastro, was going to resign to move to St. Thomas. His sorrow cut deeply and for months he prayed each evening that she would "have it good" there. This coupled with Asta's death must have made his perception of security very shaky.

One consolation that summer was the opportunity to use his reins on his donkey every day. This gave Frits a great range of freedom and speed, and he helped chase down calves and move the cattle to new pastures on a regular basis. He learned how to open and close valves for the different water troughs and knew the names of most of the cows and calves, who came on demand. Mor arranged many outings during the summer, some as far as Fredensfeld and Mt. Pleasant. The children spent a few days with the Koefoeds at Sprat Hall, playing at the beach, and there was a picnic at Ham's Bluff lighthouse with the Madsens. Mor seemed to be keeping herself very busy.

Erik and Kai with Frits who is on Violet (1918)

— Chapter Eight —

The Great War and Transfer

When he reached the age of reason, Frits was old enough to attend Lutheran Sunday school classes and begin preparations for his confirmation. His godmother Joanna Sivertsen gave Frits a big English Bible for his eighth birthday. Mor suggested that when he got a little older he would "always enjoy reading the Bible so God's word might be a lantern for his foot, and a shining light on his way." There was an after–school party with his school friends; Mor served the usual chocolate drink and Vienna cake. He received a great deal of candy from his chums, which he shared each night with the family until it was finally gone. He got dominos and a horse racing game that was very popular. The boys played so hard that his new cricket ball "went missing." One gift that did survive his early childhood was a brand new twelve–foot long cart whip.

Frits continued to work every day with Else and her chickens. One particular day while running after them, he stepped on one of Kai's little chicks and killed it. Frits was really sorry about this and arranged for a very good funeral, complete with songs. Mor arranged a small party for the family on 30 November 1915, Asta's birth day. Each child was given a little gift from among Asta's things, they took flowers to her grave and sang her favorite bed time song. It was a healthy way to deal with sorrow and to keep the children aware of how loved they all were, even in death.

Frits was earning money now, as well as earning credit with Else for tending her livestock. From his parents he got one cent for every ten cockroach eggs he collected. They also rewarded perfect scores in school. By Christmas of 1915 he had earned more than a dollar. He did not like to spend money, but he did buy each member of the family a gift for Christmas. The children each got a small allowance to cover costs of their little lunches on school days.

The Lawaetz children attended the Danish school in the Bell House on Strand Street, now home to Petersen Public Library. Its principal was Fred McFarlane, uncle of Athalie McFarlane Petersen for whom the library is now named. At lunch time Frits and his sisters would walk a half–block north to the ground floor of 45 Strand Street to have lunch with Sister Maren at the Lutheran Child Care Center, now the residence of Miguel Garcia. A drink of milk and "titty bread" cost each child one cent.

The Ebeneezer Home for Girls on Prince Street, begun by the Crown Princess Louise, where Frits's godmother was in charge, is now known as the old Queen Louise Home for Children. Sunday school was held there. Frits used his own money, one cent, to pay his Sunday school fee every other Sunday. Sister Annie Thomsen was his teacher. The cost of one cent to attend the Sunday school classes was not a small amount. Wages for field workers began at ten cents per day. That one cent equaled an hour's labor for many. Top wages for the most experienced first–class worker was twenty cents a day for a nine–hour day. Not much had changed for workers since Carl arrived on St. Croix in 1891.

Frits remembers when he was going to school there were about 150 stevedores working in Frederiksted. Before the long pier was built, cargo was brought in and out to the big ships in the roadstead by small boats called "lighters." Porter carts came up to the wharf with a lip as low as two inches off the ground so barrels of goods could be rolled off the boat right onto the cart. Then porters would run the cart down to a shopkeeper and deliver his goods directly into his warehouse. Frits says there were always hundreds of pigeons underfoot when cargo came in or sugar was getting shipped out.

"Sugar bags weighed two hundred and fifty to three hundred pounds so you know the stevedores were big, strong men. When sugar was loading, we kids knew to stay out of the way. Sugar loading went on day and night until it was done. Now all those jobs are gone."

The low level of wages was the reason for so much labor unrest in St. Croix at this time. Several attempts to form agreements with employers had already failed by 1915. A great number of employed people simply migrated to the United States. But low pay and rising prices on food caused by the Great War created pressing needs for those left behind. Out of the unrest emerged several articulate leaders calling for a united front, among them was a teacher, David Hamilton Jackson. Governor Helweg–Larsen, most employers, and many black leaders and politicians were against a union, fearing a change in power from themselves to these upstarts. The labor leaders raised funds and sent D.H. Jackson to Denmark to petition for a raise in the wage scale, the right to assemble, and a free press in English. All the time he was there, island planters kept cabling Danish officials, urging them to ignore Jackson. When Jackson returned, he called for a general strike in January.

Despite the looming threat of strike by the agricultural workers, Christmas of 1915 was exciting as usual for Frits and his family with a family tree, a church tree and their Christmas second day party for Little La Grange village workers and families. Commander Henri Konow on the warship *Valkyrien* came to St. Croix with a party of Danish officials looking over the islands with a view to selling them (again) to the United States. During Christmas holidays the family attended a reception on board *Valkyrien* and watched the lowering of the Dannebrog with full honors at sunset. All the children attending were given a ship's ribbon to wear.

The *Valkyrien* stayed on through the strike called by Jackson, which first saw government and private employees in the towns striking in sympathy with the agricultural workers. Hundreds of striking workers who left or were evicted from their estates went to stay with family members or sought shelter in the churches.

Hundreds more workers and their families were said to have set up camping sites along the west end road from Frederiksted to Ham's Bluff lighthouse, an event which Frits, then just eight years old, does not recall. Little La Grange and Jolly Hill did not grow cane, and their help did not strike, and so they were not affected directly by the strike.

As the strike wore on through January, sympathetic striking town workers returned to their desks. Owners of sugar cane estates began to feel the pressure as the cane harvest, which usually started in January, did not begin. As a result of continuing negotiations, Jackson's strike finally ended in March when the most experienced worker's pay was raised from twenty cents a day to thirty cents. Overtime rate was set at four cents an hour. It was a big victory for the workers. Ever since, Liberty Day, as it is known, has been celebrated on 1 November in Grove Place, an estate bought by the unions. Sympathetic to the homesick young *Valkyrien* sailors, Far and Mor threw a big picnic for those who had been quartered at the Frederiksted fort during the strike.

When the end of his third year exams were held in March, Frits came in second, again to Ralph Skeoch; he was very disappointed. During spring break, Frits joined Joe Bromstaff and Far in rounding up sick calves infected with lungworm. If left untreated the calves would die. Far had boarded up and sealed one of the entries to the ground floor level of their animal mill. The other entry was nearly closed off as well, leaving a small space where a pipe could protrude to allow Joe to breathe fresh air. Then Far set pots of tar and water to boiling within the mill and shut Joe up in there with the ailing calves. The steaming water and tar filled the air and had to be breathed in, at least by the stupefied calves. Joe used the pipe to avoid breathing toxic fumes himself. Finally when a calf would begin coughing, Joe would yell and Frits and Far quickly unwrapped the entry to haul out the calf. Frits would hold the calf's head so that it could fully cough out the worms from its system and begin to recover. Hard work and ugly, it paid off with nearly one hundred per cent recovery. After that it did not seem so bad to have to clean infected hooves. In later years, Far's innovative treatment of steam and tar was adopted in Denmark. His brother–in–law, Professor H. George Zeuthen, wrote asking about Far's procedure and about that of treating spontaneous abortions in cattle. Zeuthen and another professor, Frederik L. Bang, tested the tar and steam treatment and released the information throughout the region, crediting Far for the system. Professor Bang would become famous for his treatment of spontaneous abortions, known today worldwide as "Bangs Disease."

When spring break was over, Kai began school. School got tougher, as Frits was now required to learn Danish. As much as the children were formed by the strict teachings of their Far, they also had the benefit of Mor's education and travels about Europe. She had great firsthand experience. In 1889, as a single lady, Mor had traveled through Germany with two of her aunts; in 1894 she went to St. Petersburg with her best friend, Ib, and her husband, steamship captain Thidemann. In 1896 Marie and the Thidemanns toured the Mediterranean and the Black Sea for three months. She had studied art for many years and loved to paint the landscapes of St. Croix. This knowledge, too, went into the shaping of the children.

Not all their time was spent on work. Frits recalls that he and Kai were typical brothers, "often having bad fights but many times in the evening after prayers, they would jump into their big bed for a crazy wrestling session. When little Erik climbed up, the house rollicked with laughter." Frits continued to have his eyes treated regularly with "boric water," a cleansing solution. There seems never to have been a diagnosis of this eye problem, but it may well have been due to Frits's constant exposure to dust in the yard and on the roads, and the fecal matter in it from livestock — chickens, goats, donkeys, horses and cattle. Possibly trachoma, it may well have been a problem for many if not most people in that time.

Conversations that summer of 1916 included speculation on whether King Christian X would really sell the islands to the United States. It seemed a natural result, given the Great War; Germany's big Hamburg–American Line was a strong presence in St. Thomas; German submarines were prowling the Caribbean, threatening shipping in the Panama Canal with their presence. It was a matter of time, people thought, before Germany tried to take over these strategic islands. Neither Denmark nor the United States were in favor of that. The treaty to buy easily passed the United States Congress on 4 August 1916.

Another event that summer of 1916 was when the Tornoe twins, Bodil and Annette, spent ten days at Little La Grange. The families were very close friends. Mr. Tornoe was manager of the bank created in 1904 by the Danish government, located on the corner of Strand Street and Customs House Lane in Frederiksted. Above it was the Danish Club. The girls, Kai's age, came for a romp in the country, joining easily in playing cricket every afternoon, and hiking through the hills, catching shrimps and eels, and collecting mangoes. During that same summer, Frits began working with his father at the monthly weighing of milk. He also managed to get infested three times with clutches of chiggers' eggs. One encounter left him with a deep clutch festering between his toes, which had to be gouged out in the hospital. His mother said that his howls could be heard for miles around, and he was bedridden again for a few days. Almost nine, he was still glad his mother had time to read stories while his foot healed.

Family friends
Bodil and Annette Tornoe, 1914

His birthday that year was a day of constant downpour, followed by a major hurricane on 9 October 1916. All schools were closed down for fourteen days. Roofs were torn off, trees uprooted, and crops were destroyed in the fields. Materials from the Catholic school at Baron's Spot were found as far as five miles away. Jolly Hill gut which passed between their house and the main road had twelve feet of water. Frits thought it was great fun having to climb across the gut on felled trees. The storm also destroyed or eliminated most native bees. Because of this, there were several years of very meager crops at Little La Grange and Jolly Hill. The schooner *Vigilant* sank in Christiansted harbor, but the crew of the Danish warship *Valkyrien* helped pull her out and clean her up so the 126 year old ship could sail again. Mor went to Christiansted and was impressed with the massive amount of damage. While waiting for school to reopen Frits took one of the bathtubs over to the gut for sailing but the tub got away and sailed off. It was finally found later washed up in Jumbie Bush down back of town near the fort. Until the 1950s bathing at Little La Grange was done in the back room early each morning, with water boiled on the grate in the kitchen. The toilet

Crossing the gut after the 1916 hurricane

was located in a private little building some distance to the north, past the far kitchen wall.

Recovery from the hurricane distracted people from the news that King Christian signed the sale treaty on 22 December. Because of its failing economy and bad weather, there were only about 14,901 people living on St. Croix, 959 living in St. John and 10,191 in St. Thomas. President Woodrow Wilson signed the treaty on 16 January 1917. If Mor and Far discussed the choices much, it is not recorded in Frits's baby book.

Mor, age forty–four, was now pregnant with her seventh child. Inger was born on 22 March 1917, one of the last of the Danish babies. Mor was not able to attend Transfer Day ceremonies at Fort Frederik on Saturday, 31 March, because it was pouring rain. Far took the older girls to town with him, but Frits and the younger children watched from "overgut" (dialect for "a hill north of the road") at Little La Grange. They were, he said, able to hear clearly the twenty–one gun salute for each flag, fired from both the American warship USS *Olympia* and the Danish warship *Valkyrien*. That evening the *Valkyrien* set sail for Denmark.

American ownership meant that the children departed the house early to march in the Fourth of July celebration parade and saw the American flag raised over the fort. Otherwise not much changed right away. Baby Inger was christened on Whitsunday, but remained a frail thing, constantly hospitalized. Inger never rallied; she died on 16 July, not even four months old. Mor consoled herself with the thought that she was home with Jesus and little Asta, and that eventually all of the family would meet there once again.

After Inger's death, Bodil and Annette Tornoe again spent ten days of summer at Little La Grange. They all crowded together in the two rooms assigned to the girls on the north side of the upstairs parlor. The boys shared a room next to their parents on the south side. Frits spent his last days of vacation at Ham's Bluff lighthouse, staying with Hans Christensen. The lighthouse inspector and his two daughters, Maggie and Violet Pedersen, lived there as well. Maggie and Violet gave Frits a hen. (Much later in life, Violet would marry Luis Golden.) The children devised a wild game of riding the play cart down the long steps of Ham's Bluff, and Frits got some intensive bruises, again on his legs, but they were not thought to be serious then.

After the transfer, it was said that, although the Danish service at 10:00 A.M. on Sundays was sparsely attended, the Lawaetzes of Little La Grange and the Koefoeds of Sprat Hall were always there. From time to time, Mor would take the children to hear the military band concerts on Sunday afternoons. The Danish school was closed. Mr. Nase was sent down from the states to run the American school, and Miss Helen Golden became Frits's teacher. Miss Golden, sister of Luis Golden, later took instructions and became a Catholic nun. For Frits's tenth birthday he received from his father a man–sized hoe, vegetable seeds and a plot for his own garden. After years of studying the village provisions grounds Frits could now prove what he had learned. He was delighted when Else gave him one of Trine's new piglets to keep as his own. This he felt confirmed his talents as a farmer. He still helped Else pick feed every day for her pigs.

— Chapter Nine —

We Become American Citizens

With American ownership came automobiles and soon there after entrepreneurs to offer car rides for hire. When the autos came down the dusty dirt roads, horses shied from the noise, pigeons scattered in flight. The scavenger pigeons quickly adjusted; it took years and great strength to control the horses. During the summer of 1917, Mor and Far made a trip by car to Estate Granard to see Albert Nelthropp, then on into Christiansted where Mor was able to see her friends in the Deaconess House. Frits's entire family went by hired car to church on Christmas Eve. "Our Lutheran Church was beautifully decorated," Mor wrote, "with Christmas trees and the service included old Danish Christmas hymns. After church we returned to celebrate with our own tree and gifts at home." On Christmas second day Mr. Richard Thomsen, the Lutheran pastor, gave the family a drive in his car after church. Riding about in cars remained a treat for many years.

The boys got several small play guns for gifts that year. Frits particularly was happy; he admired boys who went hunting for deer and fretted because his father wouldn't allow such hunting on his farms. The children made up a deck of cards to play Old Maid using milk bottle caps made of cardboard. Another favorite card game was Gnav. The biggest treat of the holiday season came as a surprise on New Years Day. Mor ran a battery–operated projector to show a movie film, inviting all the children from Little La Grange village, as well as Violet and Maggie Pedersen from Ham's Bluff lighthouse.

Then came declaration day. "On the 17th of January, in 1918," wrote Mor, "the American flag was raised for the first time at Little La Grange and we all become American citizens." At least she thought they did. In the 1916 treaty of cession, provision was made in article six that Danish citizens may remain living in the islands, retaining all property, and "private, municipal, and religious rights and liberties secured to them by the laws now in force." Those who remained might "preserve their citizenship in Denmark by making before a court of record, within one year from the date of the exchange of ratifications [17 January1917] a declaration of their decision to preserve such citizenship; in default of which...they shall be held to have renounced it and to have accepted citizenship in the United States. For children under eighteen years the said declaration may be made by their parents or guardians."

Carl Lawaetz's family chose to remain and become citizens. Their close friends, the Tornoes, knowing they would eventually be recalled by the bank back to Copenhagen, chose to declare to preserve Danish citizenship for themselves and their daughters. This too was the path chosen by the Danish missionary sisters Joanna Sivertsen, Annie Thomsen and Maren Knudsen (whose name was always pronounced "Sister Man.")

But the newly acquired citizenship was not quite what it seemed to be, despite the words in article six. When the first passport applications came back, islanders were defined only as "inhabitants of the Virgin Islands, entitled to the protection of the United States" not American citizens. This "nobody" status caused a major uproar for years.

Rufus S. Tucker, a civil servant with the U.S. Department of the Treasury, in his 1926 report to Congress on "Economic Conditions in the Virgin Islands" clearly stated the dissatisfaction felt in 1925. He said of article six, "The foregoing provision of the treaty was generally understood by the inhabitants of the Virgin Islands as intended to confer full United States citizenship rights upon those who did not exercise their right to retain their Danish citizenship. Subsequently, the Department of State, held that, as in the case of Porto Rico [*sic*], a specific declaration of the intent of Congress was necessary to confer full citizenship...so that, as the matter now stands, they are citizens of neither Denmark nor the United States. This situation causes much annoyance to the people....they feel that they are discriminated against through the fact that, while they were full citizens of Denmark prior to the transfer, they are not now full citizens of the United States. The State Department defines them as 'nationals'." Tucker, most of whose recommendations were adopted, said that "Inasmuch as United States citizenship was granted to all citizens of Porto Rico [*sic*] by the act of March 2, 1917, it would seem only just to grant it to the inhabitants of the Virgin Islands."

This controversy did not make much of a direct impact on the children in the Lawaetz household in 1918. Frits continued with school and his chores. He also began to collect cigarettes from Navy men and war trading cards as well. The family acquired two dogs and, as all three boys paid for the license of one, Flory, a small, brown Cruzan mutt, became their personal dog. Frits and Kai joined the newly formed Boy Scouts of America troop, training twice weekly at Frederiksted fort in smart brown uniforms. Scouts also took many field trips about the country side, one of which included a hike to the old windmill at Little La Grange. For some unrecorded reason their troop was dissolved just before summer vacation commenced.

In May, with transfer completed, nearly all of the Danish clergy and missionary sisters returned to Denmark, including Frits's godmother Joanna Sivertsen. Before she went, Joanna gave her bicycle to Frits. "It was a little big for him but he soon learned to compensate for that," Mor wrote. The Danish private school closed and Frits transferred to a school in the Moravian churchyard. It was soon named in honor of Theodore Roosevelt and American history lessons began. Mr. Harold J. Benedict was the principal, Frits recalls, a man who wore a wooden leg as a result of his war injuries. He taught the boys American baseball in the fields north of town. This game soon became the major passion of westend boys.

Nineteen–eighteen was a great year for baseball, but the islands were just about in the middle of a four–year drought, as the weather had been running dry since the horrendous hurricane of 1916. The bumper crops of 1916–17 were a distant memory. Despite the worries this must have stirred up for dairy farming, the family still had some fun. There were three other very special car trips during 1918, as special as their first trip to church on Christmas Eve. Mor was delighted with a summer visit to the Tornoes, who were vacationing at Castle Coakley. Bodil and Annette, the Tornoe twins, stayed at Little La Grange several times before they moved to St. Thomas that year. Frits says today that Bodil was the best girl cricket ball player he ever met. "Although she is right handed in all other things," Frits says, "she played ball with her left and could out bowl and out pitch most of the boys." Frits consoles himself with the fact that he could pitch a ball higher. Time was spent each Saturday on Danish lessons taught by Mor, and this year Louise Andreasen from La Grange Estate joined him, also preparing for secondary school in Denmark.

Frits learned to develop film in 1918 from his mother. Perhaps Joanna Sivertsen had made Mor a gift of her own camera and developing equipment before she left for Denmark. Mor converted the storeroom on the second floor into a darkroom, suitable for developing the sensitive glass plates. Mor wrote that Frits was a great help with the film in the evening, "possibly because he knew he could expect to receive some of the ice bought for the developing." The old pictures still around show a high measure of skill in both shooting and developing.

The Americans set up a major vaccination program and everyone got shots to prevent smallpox. On 11 November 1918, Mor entered in Frits's baby book the fact that "the terrible world war finally ended that had been going on since August 4th, 1914."

Frits contracted Spanish flu in November; he was not alone but was lucky in that his was a mild case. Island schools closed fourteen days early at Christmas break due to the flu, which overall killed a half million Americans out of a total population of 103 million. Worldwide, the Spanish flu killed twenty–two million people, leaving many survivors with tuberculosis, heart problems and high blood pressure. That Christmas Frits helped his father cut and share out the beef for the village party on the estate's front lawn. School opening was further delayed until 20 January, but the boys and Louise continued their weekly Danish classes with Mor.

While the drought was still ongoing, the Lawaetz boys incurred the wrath of Carl in such a way that it is still vivid in Frits's mind today. They had gone with their dog Flory looking for an easy place to pen up their goats and came across a roofless old ruin on the property. They began cleaning it out and found a substantial bee hive growing there that had to go. Frits and Kai were familiar with gathering honey so they started a smoky fire, forcing the bees to abandon their hive. The smoking was going along well, except it was seen and reported to Far. He was furious. The boys had been told never to light fires in dry times for even one spark could fly and ignite the land for miles around. Far told his sons, "if you can't learn from one end, you will learn from the other." All three boys had to march upstairs and lie across their bed to take as many lashes as their years. Frits went first and got his twelve, near tears from the stinging and humiliation. Kai got ten, and next was little six year old Erik, who might have been spared except he ran to avoid the licking. Far told the boys they should "never run from the wrong you do, pay the consequences."

In March 1919, Mor and Far celebrated their joint birthdays, she forty–six and he fifty–four, as a one–hundred year anniversary. All the Lawaetz children took a day off from school and a large number of photographs were taken.

There was so much rain in May that the aqueduct to La Grange was damaged and Lawaetz's road washed out. Since the road was maintained by the estate owner, this was an unwanted expense. Large trees floated easily down the overflowing gut, and two fell across the gut and road by the village. A man and his horse drowned at the entrance to town by "Pond Bush," Frits remembers. The strength of weather often dominates memories in the tropics.

The famous one–hundred–year birthday: Carl turned 54 and Marie turned 46. (L–R) Dentist Hark, Bingham Hark (standing), Sister Maren, Kai (standing), Mrs. Hark, Carl, Anna (standing), Erik, Marie, Frits, Else (standing), ____, and Mrs. and Mr. Friis of Mt. Victory

In June the children's world completely changed once again. Their beloved nana, Dorothea James, left the family after eleven years, to move to the United States. She had first come when Frits was six months old, living all that time in the small apartment north of the house, once the site of the original kitchen for Little La Grange. Her departure was a major wrenching for everyone. This spring also was Frits's last time at Roosevelt school for he was now studying under a full–time tutor in preparation for his transfer to high school in Denmark. The family thought at one time about sending him to the United States to live with one of Mor's relatives, but news of race riots across America may have discouraged that possibility. His friends Selwyn Fleming, Ralph Skeoch, Ira Ross, Claude Richards and Otis Browne were preparing to go to America for their higher studies. At this time St. Croix's highest grade level was eighth; Danish law had required students attend up to the age of thirteen. Those going into trade joined a business as apprentices; children with family in St. Thomas were sent there for high school; the rest went abroad. Many, including Bodil, went to boarding school in Antigua, as did Rex Hodge and the Armstrong and Canegata boys. On the bright side of that summer of changes, Else gave Frits a goat of his own in thanks for his hard work with her livestock. Frits named him Tommylang and taught him many tricks.

Kai and Frits with their goats, circa 1921

— Chapter Ten —

Preparations for School Abroad

With most Danish speaking people repatriated to Denmark, there was need for another person to prepare Frits and the other children in Danish, so a Miss Susan Jensen was sent out from Denmark. Unfortunately she somehow got on a fast ship to Jamaica. An old saying goes, "you can't get here from there." In this case it was quite true. The wind and currents made it too expensive to maneuver a sailing ship eastwards in the Caribbean in that era. Miss Jensen had to take another ship from Jamaica up the eastern seaboard to New York and then come by steamer back down the coast to St. Croix. School with Miss Jensen did not begin until the new year. Mor noted that Frits could read Danish all right, but he had difficulty with the three different pronunciations of the letter "a."

Financially things had improved a bit. With the cessation of war, shipping was safe again. Far sold nineteen cattle to a Puerto Rican man at the end of 1919. Frits was very proud that he could help drive them, first to La Grange where the cattle were weighed, then, using his twelve–foot long cart whip to keep them in line, to dockside where they were lifted on board. With the proceeds Far bought the boys a new spring bed for Christmas, a two–horse phaeton for his wife, and another horse, which they named King George, to work with Queen Mary. Far also invested in his first

Senepol bull. Bromley Nelthropp was so sure of its value he offered to buy back any excess calves.

These days were a boy's delight. There were wonderful horse races to attend on holidays; donkey races were arranged just for fun; and the sea and Jolly Hill gut were there for swimming. Trees along the river banks were laden with sweet fruits, free to those who would collect them. There were picnics and ball games with friends, bike trips, and work to do. Pictures were being shown at the movie house in Frederiksted; often a huge navy ship was in port, bringing sailors who were happy to talk to and impress small boys. There was always Tommylang and other goats around to put in harness for cart racing. And when he thought Mor wasn't around, Frits was known to ride his donkey from the hillside down through the dining room for a shortcut to his pen.

Just before Christmas of 1920, Far's top milkman, Thomas Capstairs, lost his hand in an accident. For the rest of his vacation, Frits took over some of his milking chores that began at 4:00 A.M. Frits spent milking time talking with Thomas Ashby, the milk cart driver. Ashby had been the sole exception to military curfew during the 1916 labor strike because he delivered milk. He was full of stories about sugar cane mill work and the labor strike.

Despite his extra work, Frits was expected to maintain high standards in his Danish lessons. He also kept up his provision grounds. Frits had a grand crop of vegetables that year, selling more than eighty pounds of peas and potatoes to his family. He was not as successful with his pigs. They were allowed to run loose and became quite wild. Frits finally had to put ox rings in their noses to prevent them from rooting all over the yards. Thomas Capstairs died late in January and Frits continued milking on weekends during school. Life wasn't all work however. He spent Easter vacation at Mt. Pleasant with his close friends, Rudolf and Jeff Nordby.

On the Fourth of July 1921, the children had a wonderful day at the races at Mannings Bay, attending with their mother and visiting with many of their friends. Upon arriving home they learned that Far had shot the children's two dogs because Miss Jensen, the tutor who lived in the north bedroom, complained so much about their night howling. The boys were stunned; Flory had not only been their close, loving companion but the source of many puppies which the boys loved to raise. Forgiving Miss Jensen was a very a hard thing to do. Far's right to take such an action was never questioned.

— Chapter Eleven —

Final Days Before Departure

Frits began dancing lessons at the English church parsonage during the summer of 1921. Classes were taught by the minister's wife, Mrs. Smith. Ralph Skeoch, Norman Coulter and Selwyn Fleming also attended; Frits enjoyed it thoroughly. Too soon for Frits, Ralph and Norman left to go to school in the states, followed soon after by another friend, Bingham Hark, the dentist's son. It left a large gap in Frits's life. Frits said that he and his friends kept in touch by mail over many years.

The previous year Anna, Else and Kai had spent part of the summer in St. Thomas with the Tornoes. This summer Anna and Else went. Frits, lonesome for friends, wished he could go as well. There were still some boys around though, and Frits, Kai and Erik would collect John Merwin from Sprat Hall and Sven and Hans Jensen from Big La Grange and go swimming in the sea. Kai recalls one crazy day, after the boys found a dead dog, when Frits dared to swim far out to sea to tie the dog onto the shark bait barrel. Luckily for Frits no shark was tempted while he swam out with the dog, but the fear and excitement were exhilarating for the boys. Sharks were drawn to the area by waste and blood from the abattoir that was located until the 1950s just south of the present day fish market. The stone floor is all that remains today. Usually fishermen took a dead animal out by boat and attached it to the old rum barrel anchored for that purpose. A line ran back to shore and was attached to a strong coconut tree so the shark couldn't run with the bait. After the shark drowned, it was hauled in for sale. Frits says that overnight "his" dog caught a shark running eleven and a half feet long, and he had bragging rights for a while.

Through the summer Frits still had the goats and pigs to care for, both Else's and his own, but he was not as diligent at it as Else, for Far threatened to shoot them if he didn't keep them out of the gardens.

Recalling his parents as they were in the years before he left home, Frits says "they were very happy together. I've never seen two people that were so happy together. I never heard a cross word between them except when they played chess at night. Mor adored chess and became quite good at it. She would make a move and corner Far's king. He would start in calling her all kinds of cheat and, listening from bed, we boys would take Mor's side with great enthusiasm and laughter."

Mor began mourning the departure of her children when Frits had his fourteenth birthday in 1921. It had finally been decided to send the three older ones to Denmark for advanced training. Every action became cause for thought that this might be the last time it would happen for many, many years. Mor wrote that Frits was great as the clown in the play given at the English schoolhouse. She was delighted he enjoyed his birthday. She noted he helped his father vaccinate the calves against white scour, a fatal form of dysentery. He cut wild bees nests for honey with Buddy Frayer who was allowed to go shooting deer on other plantations. After Frits recovered from a bout with dengue fever, he and Louise Andreasen, the Lawaetz's closest neighbor, began confirmation classes on Friday nights at the Lutheran church.

In October Miss Jensen got very ill and was hospitalized, so Mor taught the Danish classes until she too became ill and went into the hospital. Mor was released shortly before Christmas but Frits was the only one at home well enough to attend Christmas church services. Miss Jensen never recovered, so Frits transferred back to the Roosevelt school at Moravian yard for the balance of the eighth grade. He would ride his bike over to the Daniels house and then walk to school with Julio and Mario Daniels. There was always a ball game after classes were over, and Frits played them all: cricket, baseball, soccer. At home he and Kai would form up teams with the village kids. On days there was no school, Frits would be up at 4:00 A.M. to help with milking. Frits's cousin Ellen Thuesen arrived in April to teach Kai and Erik in Danish. She also helped Frits improve in Danish and physics before he left St. Croix.

In April 1922 Far sold sixty–one head of cattle to Rufino Ruiz in Puerto Rico, making money to pay for the children's passage to Denmark in June. During school break, Else, Frits and Anna helped Far drive the sold cattle from Little La Grange eastward on the north shore road, eighteen miles over hills to Christiansted. At the entrance to town they took Sobotker Lane to Strand Street, Frits flamboyantly displaying his expertise with his whip. The driven cattle exited Strand Street onto King Street, to pass by venerable old Government House, once the capital building for the Danish West Indies, and a short distance eastward turned into the back gate of what is now King Christian Hotel. Once weighed, the cattle had to be hoisted into the hold of the schooner taking them away. It was hard, sweaty and dangerous work for everyone.

The photo above was taken in 1963, but the process of loading livestock was essentially the same in 1922. A grownup Frits is wearing a white hat.

Finally, Frits was ready for his religious confirmation; Mor made it a momentous occasion. After eight months of preparation, he was confirmed, alone, on 28 May by Pastor Pedersen. Mor remarked that it would have been her parents' golden wedding anniversary if her father had lived. Guests for the luncheon were their pastor, Sister Maren Knudsen, the Koefoeds of Sprat Hall and the Nordbys. His special gift of a new Bible and hymnbook from Denmark could not arrive in time, so Frits was to receive them when he went to Denmark. Mor held a tea that afternoon, entertaining more of their Danish friends: the Andreasens of La Grange, the Pedersens of Ham's Bluff, Lieutenant Olsen and his family, Policeman Jensen and his family and Mr. Thornberg. Throughout the entire territory at this time only about four hundred people were left who spoke Danish. Carl and Marie Lawaetz surely knew all of them. Frits received a fine pair of field glasses from his grandmother and Aunt Asta in Copenhagen, Denmark. His parents gave him fifty kroner to buy a watch. In addition, he got a total of twenty–five dollars to purchase necessary items in Denmark. After school closed, the family made an all–day car trip with two cars nearly round the island, ending at Nordbys where Frits stayed with his friends for a last few days.

While passports were ordered, Frits and Else made decisions about their herds and flocks. Their goats were sold to the butcher, as was one of Frits's pigs. Frits's second pig and a few of Else's were given to Kai and Erik to raise until the pigs had grown a little more. The fowl were weighed and Mor bought them from her children. The children got new vaccinations; Frits got new eye drops; and suddenly, it was time to go.

Mor wrote: "Sunday June 18, 1922, around noon the truck came for our baggage. Just before lunch we had a God blessed little Andagt [devotion] where we asked the Lord to bless and take care of you three children as His children always, forever. We closed by singing, 'Always Cheerful Where and When you Leave.' This may very well be the last time we all gather together in our dearly beloved home where all you dear children were born. We don't know if you, my dear boy, after you get through with schooling in Denmark will return to help your dear father." In a stronger hand she wrote, "Just after lunch Herbert Fleming came in his car to fetch us. We all drove to town, Frederiksted, where the steamer *Marina* lay and waited for you three...."

Mor did not go aboard. She said goodbye at the dock, crossed the road and went upstairs to the balcony of the Danish Club, over the bank that Mr. Tornoe had managed until 1917. There, by using her field glasses, she could see her children and her husband very clearly. The ship's horn blew, and very quickly the steamship *Marina* disappeared from sight. Mor was devastated to think that now her children would be so far from home, "that they were leaving their parents and would be living among strangers."

Mor wrote in his baby book: "Be always straight forward and honest, loyal and trustworthy with your work. Let Jesus always be your best friend. Speak with Him about anything and never let him escape from you dear Frits and never turn your back on Him or stray. As you now have left your home, I must now take leave with this book, that has been a great pleasure for me to write, telling about all your many achievements from Date of Birth October 5, 1907, to the day you left your beloved family and home on June 18, 1922. We will miss you, our dear big boy, our little manager. May God bless you and be with you always. Your own Mor."

Far traveled as far as St. Thomas with them, where they stayed for ten days with Mr. Tornoe. Tornoe's family had departed permanently for Denmark some weeks before, and he would soon follow. On Wednesday, 28 June, the children boarded the M/S *Panama* for Liverpool. Else, sixteen, Frits, fourteen, and Anna, eighteen, did not travel alone. Sister Maren Knudsen and the Koefoed family were on the same arrangements, so, except for parting from their parents, the trip was probably wonderful for the Lawaetz children. At Liverpool they transferred by train to Harris and from there took the ferry across to Esbjerg on the west coast of Jutland. Going by train to Copenhagen, his journey from childhood over, a whole new life was beginning for Frits.

— Chapter Twelve —

Polishing the Rough Edges

In Copenhagen Else and Anna set up home base at Aunt Asta and Uncle Ejnar's house. Anna went into training as a nurse. Else, soon to be seventeen, chose to apprentice in housekeeping. Frits picked up his new Bible and hymnbook and was sent for the summer months to Far's cousin Otto, to work on his dairy farm at Holmegaard. He also had to adjust to the weather. Midsummer in Denmark is seldom warm like the tropics. In St. Croix, summer weather is eighty–five to ninety degrees Fahrenheit. Denmark's summer temperatures are rarely more than sixty–eight degrees during the day. Another adjustment was the sheer number of people. Not only were there millions of Danes (many of them relatives), but in summer, farm workers were supplemented with migrant laborers come for harvest. For Europeans, Frits was an attractive oddity, taller than most, muscular and tanned, with a very strange Danish accent. They called him "Store Neger" (big Negro), because he came from the West Indies, or "American cowboy." He recalls going on a trip to the zoo, carrying his twelve–foot long cart whip, playing the role of cowboy to an audience of boys his age. When challenged as to whether he could really throw the whip, Frits had the boys step back and began lashing and snapping and cracking. Howler monkeys nearby began to screech and howl; the more Frits lashed, the louder they got. Soon every monkey in the park was yelling or thumping and racing up and down and across their cages. Within minutes a park attendant came yelling; Frits and the boys quickly departed after many apologies.

When school terms began, Frits moved to Stenhus Scholen, a boarding school. The headmaster was an old childhood friend of his father's. Stenhus means "stone house" in Danish. His boarding school was a widespread number of sturdy oblong, unadorned buildings surrounded by open fields near the town of Holbeck. Holbeck lies at fifty–six degrees latitude, about eleven degrees short of the Arctic Circle; the weather, Frits recalls, was never warm. His short pants and high folded–over stockings were replaced with long woolen trousers, a foreign material to him. Despite layers and layers of clothing, that first winter he suffered terribly from the frigid air. Another concern that bothered him deeply was how much farther advanced the Danish boys were in learning. Other students had already studied Swedish and German and were starting on French, while he was still learning Danish. They also had many years over him in studying math and sciences. And the school was big, so big that Frits felt lost. Although he did not recognize it, Frits was also stunned by culture shock. His parents and their older friends spoke Danish socially in St. Croix, so he was used to hearing it, but as the dominant language now, it was vastly different from the soft Crucian dialect of his playmates and neighbors. In Denmark those early years, he saw no people of color, no black, brown or cocoa–colored skins. He heard no Hispanic voices, no quelbe music, no stories or laughter drifting on warm, humid night air. He missed the creaks of carts and horses working around the calls of the stevedores loading sugar sacks onto ships. Those first months were very hard. Then he joined Boy Scouts again and was on the soccer team. He participated in track and won a one hundred meter track race once, so his mood improved.

Frits was grateful when Christmas came; he took a train to Copenhagen to stay with Asta and Ejnar. There he was reunited with his sisters and with the Tornoe family who had returned to Denmark permanently that year. Particularly, he got to visit with Bodil, and she agreed to write to him at school. Bodil had charmed

Frits for as long as he could remember. She was petite, clever, sharp witted and funny, and could easily beat him at the cricket bowling pitch. When he was thirteen Frits had given her a little kiss which made her giggle, and he promised her that one day they would marry. Returning to Stenhus, Frits kept a picture of her on his desk and told all his school friends that this beautiful girl would one day be his wife. It was not so hard to return to Stenhus when Bodil was living in Denmark too. They wrote little letters back and forth. Happier, the next three years passed rapidly for Frits. Frits spent summers working on cousin Otto's farm; holidays were passed in Copenhagen seeing Bodil. Towards the end of his senior year, it was time for Frits to take the Danish REAL exam. He had no intention of going on to junior college, but the exam was required and he did quite well, he remembers. He began serious preparation for his apprenticeship by applying to farms seeking long–term help.

Bodil waits for her turn at croquet (circa 1922)

— Chapter Thirteen —

On His Own

Cousin Otto expected Frits to start his apprentice time with him and was quite hurt when Frits said he was striking out on his own. Frits explained that he felt awkward with all the Lawaetz family known as big farmers in Denmark, that he didn't want his first real working credentials to state that Frits Lawaetz came recommended by a relative. He felt he needed to establish his own credibility, and he wanted to go where no one knew the family name. The school set up a correspondence for him with a farmer who, for all purposes, was located at the end of the world on the northeast side of the western island of Jutland. Because of his young age and limited knowledge of Danish agriculture, he was hired on as the lowest of the apprentice numbers for nine dollars a month plus a room and meals.

In August 1925, Frits left dazzling Copenhagen for Jutland. He traveled by train across land and by ferry across the sea, and the two hundred mile trip took all day. When he arrived at Allingabro near midnight, Frits was the only one to get off the train. A single model T Ford stood silently in the gloom of the midnight sky. After asking for directions to Mr. Hoijlund's farm, he requested a lift since, as the man said, the farm was out in no–man's land. When he arrived at Hoijlund's, the farmer had to be awakened. He, in turn, roused his wife who made Frits a sandwich and a cup of coffee before showing him to his bunk.

His first night spent with total strangers might have been

*Frits, at left, in Jutland on Mr. Hoijlund's farm.
Farm clothes were not stylish in 1925.*

amusing, except Frits was only a boy, not yet eighteen. Each worker was assigned a small strip of room in an unheated building. And in each room was a box–like bed with a mattress made of rye trash. The bed was covered with sheets and a quilt stuffed full of sea weed. Frits jokes now that the weight of that sea weed quilt is why his shoes are all worn down on one side — the thing weighed a ton and kept his feet splayed. His first night there he got very little sleep. He figures that nobody had slept in that bunk for a very long time; it was full of mice in the straw, and whether they were making love or fighting, he never knew, but all night long they were moving and all night long he shook them out. Soon the floor was rampageous with running mice. At 4:30 in the morning he heard sounds of men running around the yard and finally fell asleep. When he woke up he had to break the ice in his water pitcher to wash his face and hands. Although Frits had risen early nearly every day of his life, the boss told him he had "let him rest a little late that morning because it was his first day. Thereafter he had to report to the stables at 4:30 in the morning like all the rest." In that part of Denmark, the summer sun sets at nearly 10:00 P.M. and comes up again about 4:30 A.M., so that was not a hardship for Frits. The farm workday usually ended about 8:00 P.M. in harvest time.

Another memory from that first job stays clearly in his mind today. Putting on his farm boots in winter became the hardest thing to do each morning, he said, "because if your boots got wet during the day they froze at night. They were long boots up to your knee and had a half–inch wooden sole between your foot and the bottom of the boot and galvanized steel tipped, all made so they would last a lifetime. The only way to get that frozen boot on was to stand and hit the toe against the wall with all your might, driving the foot into the shoe little bit by little."

His first assignment was in the field department which included "working on everything dealing with plowing and harrowing potatoes, grain and beets. Nothing to do with the livestock except taking care of your own horses." On his second morning, as expected, he went to clean out the stable and groom his horse. As last man, he got the weakest span of horses that could scarcely pull a plow. At 5:30 A.M. the crew went into the farmhouse for breakfast. "They served food," Frits remembers, "that stuck to your ribs — black bread mixed with fresh milk and a kind of coffee that was not real coffee but was very good tasting. It put strength in you and made you strong, because there was no end to the work."

It was at mealtimes that he learned the second thing about being the lowest man on the crew. At dinner time, as lowest man, he had to sit at the far end of the table. "And of course when the food comes, then the big dish comes first to the foreman. He took first choice, and it passed back and forth down the line. If it was chicken and rice, when it reached to me, well, I could smell the chicken in the rice but there ain't no chicken left."

Frits's first work was putting potatoes into keels or coolers to store until winter when they had to be sorted and classified by weight and size. Any with spots or black had to be thrown away separately or given to the pigs. Frits recalls it was bitter cold out there, with the North Sea wind always blowing. And this was August. "The owner came by and saw me and remarked, 'But you're all blue.' I said I didn't have any more clothes left to put on."

And it was unlikely that he could afford to buy any on his nine dollar monthly pay. So Mr. Hoijlund went and got a skin jacket for him to use, because the boy really was freezing. Frits remembers that kindness. That winter, when he was working far out at the end of the farm, an old lady came along by a little hedge and peeped in at Frits. Finally she came over to a haystack secretively so nobody could see her and called for him to come there. Frits recalled that "she had brought a big hunk of cake and five wonderful hot cups of coffee for me. She said she had been watching me there working hard in the terrible weather and felt she just had to do something." Frits said it did a lot for his religious views to be living among those kind people. "I really liked the boss; he worked us hard but always fair." He and his wife had eleven children and apparently Frits hit off sparks with the baby sitter, because years later one of those children would recount a family story of Frits receiving fatherly advice from the boss on New Year's eve about his romantic advances towards the sitter, while Frits allegedly had the girl of their discussion hiding under his bed at that moment. Frits denies this, but not the fact that he set up a distillery during his time there.

While Frits was teaching the Jutlanders about ingenuity, he was learning constantly. One lesson he never forgot was giving direction properly. He was sorely berated once by the boss for saying he left the wagon on the "right" side of the barn. Unclear directions caused extra work and annoyance, he learned. Thereafter Frits used north, east or whichever applied, but he noticed later on in life that he could never get his wife to accept any such direction in his house.

After six months, at option time, Frits chose to train in the dairy. His boss offered him the part of foreman and Frits, shocked, reminded him, "I'm only a kid. I'm only eighteen years old." But the boss said he had been watching Frits all winter, helping the foreman and his assistant in the barn, and he wanted to give him the job. Well, Frits wasn't about to explain that the reason he was in the barn all his free time was because it was the only warm place besides the kitchen. His own small room was always ice cold, good just for sleeping. But Frits also loved the cattle and could talk with the crew easily about various concerns and treatments and it showed. Frits became the foreman for the next six–month period and he was very pleased.

Part of his dairy work was driving milk wagons to the cooperative separator station. "Ours was the biggest farm, so along the route we picked up another hundred gallons from one little farmer or the other, because they didn't have the time or manpower to go there themselves. Every can had its name and number so it was simple work." Along his route farmers wives made sure that cheerful, good–looking Frits always got a cup of coffee or a little piece of cake. Frits loved that route, he said it was very photogenic. On the way back he delivered the skimmed milk back to the different farms. When their farm animals contracted hoof and mouth disease Frits was the only worker allowed to leave the farm for six weeks to carry the milk to the station. The use of the milk was restricted as well, and there were more steps in the processing, but the disease soon passed.

Finally it was coming around to October again, time for new contracts to be signed. And Frits wanted to move on to a bigger place. "Danish farm newspapers carried a long list of people who were looking for new apprentices, so we would sit in our bunkhouse, all the workers, and talk about the different offers. And if anyone had served there or heard about it, he would talk about the three most important things to apprentices: number one, is the boss known as a good farmer? Is he demanding of good work? Number two, you ask about the food because that's part of your salary and what you want is good food. Last is, what about the equipment and the horses?"

The next step, Frits said, once a prospect has been chosen, is to get a recommendation from your boss. "And that boss, if it applies, might say, he's sorry he cannot do it because there were many times he had to call your attention to coming late, and so on. So he will say the best he can do is give you a statement that you worked for him. If that was all you got, then forget it, because you wouldn't even get picked. If you got a good recommendation then you send it on to the farmer who selects a list from all his applicants based on the reputation of the farmer writing it and the rating he gives you. If you are selected, you get a letter saying he expects you to report at six o'clock on the day after you leave your old job, and however you do it, you get there if you've got to drive all night. Once you arrive you have two weeks to prove you can merit the rating number he gives you."

Frits was fortunate in his application. When he arrived at the new farm two hundred miles away, his rating earned him the number three slot. Number one was reserved on every farm for a man who knew the farm inside out, often a former apprentice employee. So Frits had to prove himself as the third from the top in that six–month slot. "For the next two weeks," Frits says, "it was blood and sweat. The fields were to be plowed, and the owner knew personally just how long it took to close a row and cover the entire field. When he arrived on horseback every line had to be squared and true, it was unacceptable to have even one small skip in a row; you had to start again. Here is where it made a big difference whether you got the higher numbered horse or not."

While the boss was doing his analyzing, he asked Frits if he would be willing, should one of his foremen at the dairy get sick, to get up at 3:00 in the morning and do the foreman's work. It was still testing time so Frits was willing, and the foreman did get sick. For a time Frits had to work from 3:00 in the morning 'til 7:00 in the evening, earning just an extra ten cents a day. There was also an opportunity to work during rest break hours for ten cents more, and Frits took that too. He said, "Working in the dairy was not a hardship. All the milkers were women, mostly young, Polish women and I enjoyed it." By the end of the two weeks of evaluation, Frits was, as he said, "in his number;" he kept his high rating.

— Chapter Fourteen —

Team Work and Tempers

The new farm was a larger operation. Customarily, every summer, both before and after the Great War of 1914–1918, young people came up to Denmark from Poland to work. They would come with a rating number, and a labor society in Denmark placed them at different farms where the need for help and the need for work merged. "A lot of the women," Frits says, "were beautiful, and strong you know. Milking isn't so easy as you think. Many a man gets cramps in their arms, but you develop that special muscle. And they were good at that. And they were also good working in the field with sugar beets, which Poland [also] grew well."

Frits found out during his apprentice years that he really did like to fight. Unlike his boarding school days where much was accomplished by intimidation, on the farm a young man had to fight with his fists. Fights started easily with something done or said, and usually finished just as quickly. Some were simply showing off for the girls. But occasionally a more serious fight would develop. Frits explains that when a grudge began to build up over time, or a man felt he was being singled out for harsher treatment, it had to be seriously settled. "Farm animals and farm equipment are both powerful and dangerous. A worker had to know without any doubt that his coworker would come to his assistance immediately. If a man was working with cattle in a yard and suddenly got penned in or maybe a chance of being gouged to death, he had to have a guy with him that'll take a chance to help."

There were several times Frits experienced situations where settling the issue came near to getting out of control. In one memorable conflict Frits remembers there was a new foreman, a big fellow, from the German border. He was bossy, interfering with their free time, unreasonable, and as Frits said, "I didn't like him, period. Coming home one night with a friend of mine about one o'clock, a beautiful moonlit night, I say, 'You know what? I'm going to the crib house and I'm going to burn his bedroom.' He said, 'You're crazy!' I said, 'Well, I can't beat him because he's about twice my size, but he needs to get a little lesson.' My buddy, he was reluctant to burn the mattress, and we settled on another thing. We lassoed this heifer and brought it in the crib house where this guy had a room of his own — the room wasn't more than about ten by ten feet — shoved it in and slammed the door. Well, there was a big commotion in there, everything was going on, a chair knocked down and we were killing ourselves with laughter." Quickly, the boys knew they had to get out of sight and went to hide behind one of the big barns. Frits said they saw the fellow come out carrying what looked like a three–foot piece of pipe with him. He would have killed Frits if he caught him then, because he went straight to Frits's bunk about five hundred feet away. So the two young friends turned and walked across the farm into the fields and came back, as if for the first time. "We didn't fool him, he knew right off the bat that he chose the right bed. We circled around but he was all over, blocking our way, but not catching us." Finally the boys agreed that they only had an hour and a half to sleep before rising at 4:30 so they agreed to offer him their word of honor they would not let anybody know what they had done. "Save his face for him you know, so the lads would still respect him and take orders. And we promised to send one of our girlfriends over to fix up the mess." So the deal was made and they all kept their word, but thereafter every time there was particularly dirty job, Frits was given it.

Frits settled another problem differently. One of his bunk mates was a minister's son and, according to Frits, a spineless liar. "He didn't mix up much with the rest of us that were rowdy, but would still cause trouble for everyone. Whatever happened, the other guy got blamed and this pastor's son was defended by the foreman or the boss." So that wasn't going down well with Frits. He knew what was right from wrong, and the way things were going would never make a man out of this fellow. Frits determined to be the one to change that. One night when the moon was full and beautiful, Frits asked him to come out and finish a fight between them, but Frits was rebuffed and the door was locked against him. Frits decided there was still one way left to get at him — through the window. Frits collected his knife and a drum barrel to stand upon. Putting the knife in his mouth he began to slide down into the room through the window. "Well, when he saw my head come through there with this knife, he didn't hesitate one minute. He went flying — now at that time we only slept in nightshirts — and he went through that door like a bullet. You could see his footprints in the snow running over to a group of trees about five hundred feet from the bunkhouse. A little forest, I couldn't follow him in there. Soon I started to worry that I might cause the death of this man because he ain't look to come back. So I sent my roommate who coaxed him back." But the man just didn't respect Frits, or so he thought, and Frits said he didn't think the place was big enough for the two of them. Finally, some weeks later, the pastor's son took off. The rest of Frits's apprenticeship rolled on, full of choices of fun mixed with seriously hard work, until in 1927 it was time for Frits to pack up. His apprenticeship time was over and he wanted to go home; Frits had not seen his parents or Little La Grange for five long years.

Frits left his last job a month early, in August 1927, because his mother was arriving to enroll Erik in Stenhus. It was Mor's first visit back to Denmark since 1913, so many members of the family gathered to visit. Frits got to see Bodil again before leaving. Frits had fixed in his mind since he was thirteen years old that Bodil was to be his wife and, despite all the good–looking girls on the farms, nothing had changed his mind. But Frits was only nineteen, about to go home for his first adult job, with no savings at all. Bodil was seventeen, just old enough to commence nurse's training. They agreed to keep in touch. Frits and Mor returned to St. Croix on 2 October 1927. Two years later stock markets crashed and the Great Depression began.

Erik, Mor, Kai and Frits in Denmark, summer 1927

— CHAPTER FIFTEEN —

Back to the West Indies

Jobs were scarce in October 1927. The territory had yet to feel any benefits from American ownership, except the ability to emigrate easily to look for work. So many islanders were heading for New York that the population had dropped by fifteen percent since transfer. Frits worked for his father at Little La Grange for a while, but the scarcity of money was vexing; he had little to save because part of his pay was in room and board. Another problem was that, between 1921 and 1931, St. Croix suffered from the driest years in its history. Carl Lawaetz was hard hit by drought, and whatever cash money came in was used to pay wages and debt services. Everyone was affected. Per capita income in the Virgin Islands was $350 per person, really appalling when compared to Mississippi, the lowest state, with $1,216. Overall in the states, the per capita rate was $2,918, eight times higher than in the Virgin Islands. Common laborers in St. Croix were earning forty to fifty cents a day, for a nine–hour day when Ford assembly workers were earning five dollars a day. Hauling sugar might add ten cents more a day, but that was seasonal work only. During harvest, a good cutter might be able to earn a dollar and a half to a dollar and three–quarters a day, getting thirty cents for every thousand pounds cut. But Frits didn't want to cut cane; he had trained for cattle management. Unfortunately, on St. Croix, all those jobs were taken.

Two memorable events did remain in Frits's memory from those dreary days. First was the arrival of a three–engine plane which landed on the Prosperity cricket field in 1928. Just a year before, Lindbergh had flown solo across the Atlantic into Paris and enduring fame. Frits was so enthralled with the idea of flying that he borrowed five dollars and went up on the first flight with nine other people. He recalls happily, "The plane flew up and the cattle began running like crazy! All over the island people could be seen looking up at us, it was just fantastic." The second event occurred later that year when a powerful hurricane called San Felipe hit, about 11:00 P.M. on 12 September 1928. It raged for thirteen hours, followed by another forty–eight hours of torrential rains. There was ample warning from ships and other islands but little anyone could do. Frits remembers that his friend Jim Bennerson's grandmother, Mrs. Duncan, drowned at Concordia bridge because of it.

There wasn't much work for Frits in St. Croix, and he felt fortunate when a man came over to buy cattle and recommended him for work with the United Puerto Rico Sugar Company in 1929. He jumped at the chance and moved: it paid fifty dollars a month and a bunk. Frits served as a timekeeper at first and began training under the field manager, Oliver Heyn. He knew Heyn from St. Croix. Heyn's mother, Hulda, and her father, Mr. Switzer, owned Little Princesse plantation.

During his first harvest in Puerto Rico, Frits learned a new working pattern for cutting cane. Cutters would cut four rows at a time and throw the canes loose into a cart following behind them, reducing the number of times the cane was handled between field and mill. That cut down on theft as well as damage to the stalks. In St. Croix the cut canes were thrown behind the cutter, then bundled and then loaded into carts. The Puerto Rico Company also fertilized the canes heavily so that a greater yield was gained. The company was also experimenting with a new variety that would make the canes tougher for the rats. "The ratio in those days," Frits says, "was to plant four cane pieces in a hole: one for rat, one to thief, one for dry and one to harvest. It was the pattern all my life, planting cane, four to a hole." He also noticed during the depression that, in spite of many watchmen in the fields, a lot of cane was going to the poor people. "In Puerto Rico, there was a lot more trouble if someone got caught stealing cane, so they would go with the whole plant, pull it up by the roots, rather than just taking a little piece. Very wasteful. But pulling up didn't make noise you see, where if you broke off a little piece, the watchman might hear you."

Another observation was on the strength of family ties in Puerto Rico. He saw over and over again how completely an extended family of cousins and relatives cared for each other and that the elders were well respected by all. He was well received personally in their private homes, except of course when it came to young girls in the family. There were strict rules of behavior then, and girls of the family were well protected against even a little kiss! In particular, he remembers, girls were told to watch out for the cowboys who were considered to be "a little wild." Whenever he tried to spend a little time with a girl, there was sure to be an aunt or grandmother within sight. Despite his intent to marry his childhood sweetheart, Frits seemed to think he should keep practicing his flirting, certainly he showed none of his boyhood bashfulness now! There were cooks and laundresses, and shopkeepers' daughters to entertain. Even the telephone girl, who mailed his letters and gave him Bodil's in return, got full blast attention in return. Maybe it was just the natural affection and friendliness of character that made him a charmer of the ladies. His blond good looks and education didn't hurt either. Still, if the Puerto Rican girls were "off limits," there was a lot of excitement on the ranch and in the bunk house. Frits recalls fights, almost always over women, and remembers one story of infidelity he likes to tell. "An old man had a wife and two nice kids, but that wasn't enough for him and he began to run around with the telephone operator. One night, the man came home late and changed up his clothes in the front room, hoping not to wake his wife up. He got on his nightshirt, sneaked into the bedroom and crept into bed. As his eyes adjusted to the dark, he realized something was wrong. He took a little peek beside him and found his wife all cut up, blood all around, her hands wrapped around a knife. Oh God, he thought, she's committed suicide! Well, the man was beside himself, and began to pray to God that this terrible thing should never have happened, that he really loved her and was so sorry. When he was truly worked up about it and bawling, the wife opened her eyes, and said, 'Keep those promises or the next time it will be the real thing!' "

Frits spent four years in Puerto Rico, moving from timekeeper to field manager over that time. The sugar company imported cattle from time to time and was always in need of horses for part of their work. Sometime in 1930 or 1931, as Frits was involved in breaking horses, he encountered a horse that others had been unable to break. There were rumors that two men had been killed by this horse, one of them being a man who had beaten the horse so badly he knocked one of its eyes out. The owner's choice was to have the horse killed if Frits couldn't break it to saddle. A deal was struck when Frits said if he did break it, it was his horse alone. Frits had been around horses from infancy and knew that, like cattle, deer and dogs, horses worked on smell and saliva. Frits got the horse, which he named Puppy, well acquainted with his smell before he ever tried to mount him. Finally with a lot of coaxing, Frits got the horse to tolerate him on his back.

Frits and Puppy worked well as a team most of the time, despite Puppy's blind eye. But twice there was a problem: Frits, moving some cattle over a bridge, got pushed too close to a rail on Puppy's blind side; the back of Frits's hand was ripped open on the structure and took some time healing. Another time he was moving cattle down a road, when some traffic came toward them, startling Puppy on his blind side. "I tried to have Puppy move the cattle off the road, but it didn't work. Then the herd, maybe a hundred head of Zebu cattle barged in from Texas, began a stampede and just kept going. I saw the chain was up for a train, and we rode like hell up to the lead bull, and I put my hat over its eyes and turned it onto the train track. The cattle's hooves got cut up badly but Puppy kept going, down the track, until the cattle were exhausted. Just a thousand feet from town, the herd finally ran out of steam, and the stampede was over."

Puppy was such a challenge to the macho men that Frits made a bit of money when they would brag that they could ride him. Puppy threw a great number of men. "One day this boxer, champion boxer, bet me ten bucks that he could stay on, and he might have except Puppy bit him in the stomach and just ripped him off the saddle quicker than spit. Puppy always ran people out of the yard, just for spite. He could get his bridle off by rubbing a post too. But he became my horse and no one else could go near him. He was very intelligent, could somersault backwards, even knocked himself unconscious once bucking himself heels over head," says Frits. Another memory involving Puppy surfaces. "During a big strike in Puerto Rico there was a big gang out to stop the cane laborers from working and a man got killed. The gang leader's father was my foreman. The gang leader said he would continue to kill any man that tried to break the strike. I rode out on Puppy and challenged them — said, 'You may have a lot of chat to throw, but I am going through and I have a gun.' They let us pass. I didn't have any fear on that horse, and I didn't have a gun either."

Frits in 1928 with another of his horses, "Bell"

When the hurricane of 1932, San Ciprian, wiped out cane fields in

Vieques, Frits was sent there by the company to see what could be saved and Puppy went with him. He was assigned a small square little camp house of his own, with a bare light bulb hanging, powered by a small generator on the project. "When I wanted to impress the girls, Puppy would stand up on his hind legs and perform." After Frits left Vieques and returned to St. Croix, no one could handle the horse. The company said they would have to shoot Puppy if Frits didn't want him. By telephone, Frits hired a one–man sloop to bring the horse. "But there was a storm and the boat got driven off course and down to eastend. I had to go up there and swim out to the boat and bring Puppy in."

— Chapter Sixteen —

Home Again

Frits returned to St. Croix in 1933. Young and strong, he was recommended for new construction work in Estate Richmond. Some former distillers from Mississippi were investing in a rum distillery, the first to be built after Prohibition ended. Frits became assistant building foreman for the new Christiansted Distillery. Today the site is home to a cement block plant. Frits was called "Slim" then and recalls that the contractor, Charles Crowley, was exceptionally strict; no beer or liquor was allowed anywhere around his work site, earning Crowley the name of "Ice Water Charlie." Since it was such a long distance from Little La Grange, Frits boarded with Carl Petersen in Christiansted and came home on weekends. Every weekend, the young men who were still around would get together for a game of baseball, playing on the cleared cow pasture north of town, "upside of Pond Bush." When Frits left for Denmark, island boys still favored cricket and soccer, but as time passed and American influence gained sway, baseball had become the sport of choice. Mr. Benedict, Frits's old teacher, made sure the young men were well grounded in the rules. Frits feels the baseball stadium in Frederiksted should have been named in Benedict's honor because of the many boys he taught so well.

One weekend Frits arrived home to find, as usual, that Puppy had broken out of his corral and was off on his own. Frits crossed field after field calling for him and was close to giving up when he heard Puppy bawling in the tragic baying way that frightened horses do. This time Puppy had gotten himself all tangled up in barbed wire and was nearly dead. Frits had to cut every tangle to get him loose and then fought hard to get the horse to stand. Finally getting him home, Frits began treating his wounds and thirst, willing him to survive the shock. But it was too late. The half–blind horse nobody else could ride was unable to rally. Frits remembers that, "Deep into the night Puppy put his head on my shoulder. We had one last cry together and he died. It was the saddest sound I have ever heard. We went through a lot together."

As the distillery building neared completion, Frits began learning boiler work from Jacobus "Jack" Lammers. Jack later opened his famous bakery in his house in Campo Rico near Frederiksted, but this is where he started working, Frits remembers. As luck would have it, just as Frits was resigning himself to work in a factory, a new opportunity arose. The River–Fountain complex, owned by two Danes, Svend Mylner of St. Thomas and Frederik Jorgen Christensen of St. Croix, and a federal judge assigned to St. Croix named Denzil Knoll, was raising cattle and sugar cane and needed a new farm manager. Frits was offered seventy–five dollars a month and a house. As Frits said, "At last I had a manager's house." He had every single letter that Bodil Tornoe had ever written to him, and his hopes went soaring. He wrote her asking if she would come see him, and while he waited for Bodil to decide, he set to work at River.

"When I came to River the first time, I was quite a revolutionary. I tried to show these people how to do the job professionally. The common practice in St. Croix was to cut two stalks and throw it back, then another woman tied the stalks into bundles before moving it to the roadside for pickup. I wanted them to use the Puerto Rican method, cut four and throw them into a cart without tying. The women did not agree. I told them I wanted the cane fertilized, to get another year or two out of the fields. The women said it had never been done before, wouldn't be done now. They were vexatious, they baulked, they stalled. Finally we compromised: the fields got fertilized using imported fertilizer; that was the only order that made sense to them." The process of tying of cane in the field and manually moving stacks to the road side for a truck to pick up stayed. For the women it made sense because more people had work.

Another thing Frits did there was to sell fertilizer to homesteaders. The federal government had come into Bethlehem "to save the economy." Through the Virgin Islands Company (VICO), they set up the homestead program at Whim and other estates, advancing money to farmers to buy land and build homes. It was mandatory for those homesteaders to raise cane and deliver it to Bethlehem factory for milling. The small size of the plots was hard on the mortgagees, but they got to rent government plows and trucks for the heavy work.

Meantime, while waiting on Bodil's decision, Frits got another horse which he entered into local horse races set up to entertain cowboys. Races have always been important on St. Croix. The first track at Long Point off of Estate Carlton was before Frits's time. The next he remembers was at Betty's Hope. It was built in 1904 and was located where the Texaco tanks are today. World War II was responsible for closing Betty's Hope, because it was too close to the air base runway. It was replaced by the Oval , located where Markoe school now stands. Races then moved to Stoney Ground and after the war to Mannings Bay by the airfield.

Frits also found time to discuss the problems of farming and governing the island with his Far who still held a seat on the colonial council for farmers' interests, as he had done under the Danish and Navy governments. Carl Lawaetz as a landowner was also a voter, one of the four hundred or so Crucians who were eligible, less than ten percent of the population. But political changes were coming, brought about by the frustration of many who had no voting say at all. They were supported and abetted by Virgin Islanders in Exile in New York and Washington who spoke on behalf of the natives. The political climate may have been exciting, but Frits's singular goal at the moment was seeing Bodil.

Frits (second from right) and friends caught a manta ray on a rare day off.

Frits, called "Slim" in the 1930s, with a huge chicken hawk

Part II
The Cowboy Life

— Chapter Seventeen —

Responsibility at Last

It had been eight long years since Frits saw Bodil Tornoe. He wasn't sure of her feelings and was terribly afraid of being rejected. She was seventeen when they parted, just finished with secondary school. That autumn Bodil turned her full attention to qualifying as a nurse. She and Frits's sister, Else, remained in close contact, and Else faithfully had included in her letters information about all the Tornoes, including Bodil. Between 1927 and 1935, Bodil wrote many letters to Frits. Frits still has them, at least as many as survived the 1989 hurricane and near total destruction of his home. He is a little reluctant to share them and says they are in Danish anyway. For all the great size of him, toughened and battered by a cowboy's life and, even at ninety–three, all muscle, the romantic knight shines through as he refuses politely to share the most intimate letters of his life.

Bolstered by his new job at Estate River in 1935, Frits wrote to Bodil suggesting that she come down for a visit with Else who was returning home to St. Croix with her infant daughter for the first time in twelve years. Since Bodil was a nurse, he suggested, she would be a big help to Else. And maybe, he thought, he could find out if she still had any interest in him at all. Frits scrimped enough to buy her a one–way ticket; he did a lot of hunting and fishing to fill his stomach so that he could save that fare.

Else, six month old Merete, and Bodil arrived on 11 October 1935, and it was the gift of a lifetime for Frits, whose twenty–eighth birthday was just a week before. Bodil, twenty–six, was worth waiting for: she had the fine flawless ivory skin of her Viking ancestors, curly blonde hair and Baltic blue eyes. Small boned, scarcely 110 pounds, very witty and lively and most opinionated, she was perfectly beautiful. Frits was enraptured for the rest of his life. It would be some time before he would learn that Mr. Tornoe had given Bodil her return passage ticket so that she could make the trip and her decision about Frits independently. Mor said that her father had done the very same thing, thirty–three years before. Bodil found it easy to make the choice between living in thriving, cosmopolitan Copenhagen, home to one million Danes, and the little house at Estate River in St. Croix, population, one. After all, she was only interested in one man in the world, and home for her would always be where he was. The six–year long worldwide depression was finally easing by then, allowing many young couples to hope for better times. Even if it hadn't, Frits and Bodil had waited long enough.

For their wedding, Frits ordered rings made by Monroe Clendenen with his initials in the one for Bodil and hers in his ring. He did as best he could to put his little house in order. On his wedding day, since he lacked a good shower in his house he said, "I went to the home of my good friend Niels Abel and washed away my sins." The wedding took place at King's Hill Lutheran Church on 18 December 1935. The chapel was beautifully decorated with local flowers by Mor and Else. Frits's own minister had been selected to perform the service, and Carl served as his son's best man. Frits's best friend, Ralph Skeoch, was honored as the bride-giver, Else as the maid of honor. Frits recalls that Bodil was simply dressed in a white suit of clothes and looked like an angel. Actually she wore a full length satin gown of white, with a beautiful, fragile three–quarter illusion veil. Frits was decked out in a white suit and white buckskin shoes. They made a splendid couple. He recalls fondly that her response wasn't yes, it was a strong Danish ya!

The wedding party drove down to Little La Grange to prepare for the afternoon reception, to which eighty people were invited.

Frits and Bodil on their Danish–American wedding day, 18 December 1935

When his old family cook asked Bodil to show her the wedding ring, Frits realized he had not given it to her! Reaching into the pocket of his newly cleaned suit, he found to his astonishment a dollar and a dime. No rings. Later he was to consider that dollar and that dime a prediction for them that they would never want financially, but at that moment all he could think about was the disappearance of his specially made rings. He told Bodil that he got her one but had seen that it would be too loose so she would get it later. Then he raced back to River and asked his cook who had cleaned the Estate River house if she had seen the rings on the floor or anywhere; she said no but took Frits over to a little storeroom where she had dumped all the sweepings into a box. There, luckily, among dust balls and dog hairs, was the little brown envelope and his precious wedding rings.

They had a wonderful reception with all of their friends, and finally, at ten in the evening, it was time for them to go home to begin their married life together in Estate River. Friends had arranged a big sign of welcome for Bodil; new pots of flowers were everywhere. And the whole house was boarded up tight as a drum.

Every door and every window was battened down and secured as if for a hurricane. Frits said it took quite some time to batter his way in. Bodil climbed in the window as well, and they went into separate rooms to prepare to sleep. Frits pulled down their beautiful new spread and saw a huge banana in the middle of his brand new mahogany bed. If that wasn't enough to embarrass them, they found all their night clothes sewn up as well. Then out of the dark came several of their young friends and relatives, ready to party with bottles of champagne. And they stayed and stayed and wouldn't go home. Finally Frits picked up his shotgun and jammed in some bullets. Firing over their heads, he ran them all off into the guava bushes. When finally they could turn out the lights, a car horn began blasting away under their bed. It had been hooked up to a battery hidden outside. Bodil swore she'd never get married again! And she kept her word.

Their first child was born on the third floor of the Frederiksted Clinic on 5 December 1936; they named him Hans. Frits thought

Bodil, 1936

motherhood made Bodil look even more angelic than usual. That first night in the hospital, as Frits sat with Bodil after dinner watching her rest, he noticed a little mouse come out by the base of the wall and he watched it. Within seconds the mouse had climbed up the bed, slipped down the pillow case to Bodil's ear for a sniff, then jumped into the baby's cradle beside her bed. Trying not to disturb her, Frits snatched at it as it raced around the cradle, finally catching it but getting bitten in return. He kept hold and rushed it into the nearby closet to drown it in a pail of cold water. The mouse hadn't disturbed the baby, and as long as Bodil hadn't seen it, he just said, "It was nothing, go back to sleeping." As the custom of the time was a two–weeks' stay in hospital, Frits went to Frederiksted from River every day to visit his wife and new born son. He watched vigilantly for more mice until he could safely take them home.

Two years and two months later they returned to Frederiksted Clinic again, this time for the birth of Bent on 22 February 1939. Bodil got the same room as before. Only this time, two little mice came out of the wall. They didn't attempt to approach the bed though, and Frits after careful consideration, decided to fatten them up and hope they would leave his wife and baby alone. This worked quite well. Frits fed them nightly as he waited out the two–week post partum stay.

Frits and Bodil spent five happy years at River. The children learned to walk and to ride horses there and followed in the footsteps of their dad, just as Frits had done with his Far. Frits hunted wild deer for the table, as Bodil fed table scraps to fawns orphaned by nature or man. They always had dogs for company, as well as for cane–rat control. They had a little four–cylinder car to get around the island. On holidays and Sundays after church they went to Little La Grange where Mor could coddle and cherish them. Frits joined with other horsemen in organizing races. He had several race horses of his own that were successful. Only the political news from Europe disturbed them. Letters began to speak of the beginnings of another war.

Frits and Bodil with dogs and slain deer, 1936

— Chapter Eighteen —

Ward Canaday

When Frits first returned to St. Croix after working in Puerto Rico, one of the most influential people in his life began coming to St. Croix, a man called Ward M. Canaday of Toledo, Ohio. Canaday was wealthy, successful in business, a friend and advisor to President Roosevelt, and had a massive amount of practical business know–how. Canaday's first known visit came in 1933. Another was in 1936 when he stayed at the Pentheny Hotel in Christiansted. He was an invited guest to the reception planned at Government House for Harold Ickes, secretary of the Department of Interior. Just before the party, an explosion of the refrigerator's propane tank in the second–floor kitchen caused a great fire that destroyed the third floor of two Government House buildings. The Ickes reception had to be moved to the old Marine barracks on the southeast end of Christiansted. Ward Canaday was asking for directions to the old barracks when resident Betty Skeoch offered to escort him there, as she was attending the reception as well. Canaday may have been part of an investigative team sent down by President Franklin Roosevelt under his Public Works Projects Administration, one of the New Deal programs. It is well recorded that Secretary Ickes and Rexford Tugwell, who later served as governor of Puerto Rico, had been working in Puerto Rico on sugar cane labor reforms which lead to the creation in 1937 of the Popular Democratic party headed by Luis Munoz Marin. It is likely that Canaday was involved there as well.

At the time she first met Ward Canaday, Betty Skeoch's husband, Norman, was working with the Virgin Islands Company (VICO) at Estate Bethlehem, a federally–created company set up to relieve the island's chronic unemployment through industrial development. Betty later drove Canaday over to meet Eva Armstrong at her mid–island home in Estate Grange whom he had been told to see. (Eva was the mother of Douglas Armstrong who would open up the Buccaneer Hotel in 1948 and mother of twins Dicky and Harry who opened the Ford dealership in St. Croix.) Following the meeting with Mrs. Armstrong, according to Betty Skeoch, Ward Canaday became interested in buying land in St. Croix. Two thousand acres of land in the northwest hills of St. Croix comprised of about thirteen estates had been up for sale a long time when Ward Canaday stopped again at St. Croix towards the end of 1936, en route to Brazil. "Canaday was serving as a dollar–a–year man for Roosevelt at the time," Frits says. "He was going to South America to look into a housing program. A federal government man from Estate Anna's Hope agricultural station suggested that they take a drive and look at the main estate, Annaly. The place was all run down and occupied by squatters, but the price was very good at seventeen dollars an acre, and Canaday was sold."

Frits's name came up as a possible manager when Canaday talked with the president of the United Puerto Rican Sugar Company, Mr. Nadler, and asked him to suggest someone to run his new farm. Nadler asked his field superintendent Oliver Heyn where Frits was working and told him why he was interested. Oliver, who had been Frits's supervisor all the years he worked in Puerto Rico, sent Frits a telegram to prepare him for the offer. Chances are Canaday canvassed several people and Frits's name must have surfaced repeatedly. The huge River–Fountain complex Frits managed was well run, used excellent conservation practices and was the largest private sugar cane producer on island. Success gives the highest recommendation, and in 1940 an offer was made to Frits by Mr. Canaday.

Frits had to think about it. He was happy at River; Bodil loved it there. They had close ties as well. Bodil's best childhood friend, Tiny, was married to Svend Mylner, one of the owners. Erik Lawaetz, his assistant manager, was courting Jenny, daughter of Frederik Christensen, another owner. On the other hand, he thought it would be a great challenge for him to develop the place. He remembered Annaly from his childhood and how well Andrew Blackwood had kept it. He remembered the histories of Annaly Mr. Blackwood told to him and to his friend Ralph on rides home from school. "I needed assurance that Mr. Canaday would put the money into it and do it right. He not only assured me, he offered me a hundred and fifty dollars a month to do it well. We agreed to do it together."

Canaday had impressed Frits with his sound business sense, and well he should. Canaday, born in 1885, had been educated at Harvard near Boston and graduated in 1907, the year Frits was born. He first sold magazine ads for sixty dollars a month, then joined Hoosier Kitchen Cabinet Company as its advertising manager. There he pioneered the time payment plan concept of a dollar down and a dollar a week. In 1916 Willys–Overland, a privately owned car company in Toledo, Ohio, hired him. There he organized the first automobile credit company, which later became Commercial Credit of Baltimore. For years Ford's toughest competition was Willys–Overland. Canaday eventually left and established his own business, United States Advertising Company, with Willys–Overland as one of his accounts.

During the 1920s, the owner of Willys–Overland, John Willys, purchased the Curtiss Aeroplane Company; then he was appointed ambassador to Paris. Under absentee ownership the company began losing its competitive edge in the car industry and finally went into receivership. Although John Willys left his post as ambassador to turn the company around, he died before he could work out a plan. Canaday knew that the company still had great value, and its prices were competitive: four–cylinder autos were selling for $395. More important, Willys–Overland had thousands of well–trained employees who needed their jobs saved. Terrible memories of the worldwide depression beginning in 1929 was an enormous goad to succeed. With a group of friends and the widow of John Willys, Canaday scraped together $1.25 million, borrowed an equal amount, and reorganized the company in 1936. It paid off in a very big way. The company's quick conversion to war production in 1941 and Canaday's executive skill got him an exclusive contract for the manufacture of military semi–amphibious all terrain vehicles or "general purpose vehicles" that would be known worldwide as Jeeps. Between 1941 and 1945, Willys built and delivered $760 million worth of Jeeps to Europe and the Pacific, giving Allies the edge. He did it again during the Korean and Vietnam wars. Military use of the Jeep would not be replaced until 1984 with the creation of Humvees. Much of this history had yet to take place when Frits evaluated Ward Canaday, but he liked what he saw; their pact was made and stood good over the next thirty–one years.

— Chapter Nineteen —

Annaly

Frits set about repairing and replacing fences, building new cattle dips, clearing brush and fixing up the houses at Annaly to make Canaday's new farm workable. He says, "My first day of work was All Fools Day [1 April] 1940, then we got into the war and I didn't see Canaday again for three years." Frits established a system of monthly reports to Canaday, which Bodil, serving as secretary of Annaly Farms, faithfully typed each month. He set up a ledger system which justified and accounted for every item down to the least little nail. When the house was habitable, Frits and Bodil moved to Annaly with Hans and Bent and their nanny and cook, Teresa Napoleon Clarke.

Annaly is a beautiful estate now. Full–grown trees bearing lucious mangoes, avocados, soursops or limes line roadsides and pastures. Around the house and mill, Bodil created a lush landscaping of colorful bushes and flowers. In 1940 it must have been a daunting sight for her to even consider reclaiming it from its state of wild decay, but she made it her task to bring beauty and harmony back to Annaly. It took many years.

Meanwhile, the family had grave concerns about the war in Europe. so many of their family members were in jeopardy: Else and her family, Bodil's parents and all the cousins and aunts and uncles were in Denmark. Bodil's two sisters were married and lived in Bristol, England. Anna however was safe, living in Connecticut

House at Annaly in 1940

and serving as governess to Miles Merwin's children. War news was listened to faithfully. Four days after the Japanese air force bombed Pearl Harbor early on a Sunday morning, local radio stations announced the United States was at war on both fronts. It was 11 December 1941.

Despite registering early for the draft, it turned out that Frits would be unable to serve in the U.S. Armed Forces. He was thirty–four years old and had two children and a wife. He also had bad eyes and a bad leg. Bodil tried to return to work as a nurse to do her part for the war effort, but the hospital would not permit that, as she had minor children. She went to work instead for the U.S. Army at the Benedict Field Base. She served, too, as a volunteer with the Frederiksted Hospital Auxiliary and the Frederiksted Women's Club. Like her counterparts all over the country, she knitted mittens and socks and prepared bandage packs for soldiers and sailors. Frits said their home was always open to boys and girls in service during the war. Bodil's love, warmth and hospitality were known throughout the island. Frits says, "She wouldn't let a stranger get lonely as long as she had a scrap of time or food to share." Bodil also became a member of the United Servicemen's Organization and served there most of her life. She was president of the USO for a long time, he recalls. Frits says she was honored several times for her work there.

As for Frits, he signed up with the Home Guard, based in Estate Grove Place, St. Croix, and was made Captain of Company C. Training took place on the present day ball field at Grove Place. When Frits would finish training at Grove, he would come home and put his delighted sons through their paces with broomsticks. Part of the Home Guard's duty was to serve as spotters for submarines, and guardsmen patrolled the cliffs, particularly at sunrise and sunset when the subs may have thought themselves invisible. Frits, sixty years later, still has his Basic Field Manual (FM 21–50 issued 1941) on Military Discipline, Military Courtesy, and Customs of the Service. If any single document exemplifies his life, it is this. By the time he first read the manual, Frits had long been "a gentleman;" in 1941 he added "and an officer."

The manual begins:

> Section 1. Discipline.
>
> 1. a. Military dicipline [*sic*] is intelligent, willing and cheerful obedience to the will of the leader. Its basis rests on the *voluntary subordination of the individual to the welfare of the group.*
>
> 1. b. *Discipline establishes a state of mind which produces proper action and prompt cooperation under all circumstances regardless of obstacles.*
>
> 2. a. *Man* is and always will be the vital element in war. As an individual, he *is most valuable when he has developed a strong moral fiber, self–respect, self–reliance, self–confidence, and confidence in his comrades. A feeling of unity must be achieved if the group...is to function as a unit instead of a mob....competent to cope with any condition, situation, or adversary.*

The manual further stated the precepts under which all of the children Carl and Marie Lawaetz had been raised:

> Discipline is attained only by careful and systematic education and training. All types of military training which tend to develop a sense of duty, pride, and responsibility, loyalty, morale, respect, confidence, initiative, and teamwork are beneficial (and can be taught) in many different ways and by many different methods.

The rearing of children before World War I had leaned heavily on development of character and much of it had been accomplished through the apprentice system, "once a man, twice a boy." The military establishment understood those key components and addressed leadership from that perspective:

> ...common sense, good judgment, fairness and justice, high morale, pride and responsibility contribute as much to maintaining discipline as to attaining it. Good leadership, based on personality and character, is essential....the key to effective leadership is the development of respect and mutual confidence. He will leave nothing undone to promote the unit's comfort, welfare, and prestige. Loyalty and respect are developed through mutual understanding and consideration, through fairness and justice, and by sharing dangers and hardships as well as joys and sorrows.

Frits found common cause in defending his country through service in the Home Guard, because he and generations of his family before him held to the same high ideals as the leadership of the United States military and that of the United States government.

Above, Bodil around 1940. Below, Frits and Bent on "Billy." Friend Lawrence Merrill and Bodil stand by, circa 1941.

— Chapter Twenty —

The War Years

Frits's service in the Home Guard did not interfere with cattle farming. The production of milk and beef were also high priority for the military. Ward Canaday was constantly sending down experts to inspect and deliver opinions or having Frits contact them from Annaly all during the early years. He suggested raising grapes or oranges, and castor beans for oil extraction. Frits had found that Annaly's upper fields had been in castor bean production during World War I, and in fact he still has the castor bean advertising sign. Frits however, wanted the farm to excel in cattle production and persistently recommended stocking the Nelthropp breed. For many years Canaday would insist on trying other cattle crosses.

In addition to his farm interest, Ward Canaday was serious about eradicating diseases in the tropics. He had a brother who worked for Ligget Pharmaceutical, a chemical company which pioneered in antibiotics and antitoxins. Canaday may have had a financial interest in the company as well. He hired Harry Beatty to collect bugs and plants for testing by Ligget. Harry and Frits were lifelong friends, often hunting or fishing together, so when his sister's little grandson, Ken Abel, was troubled by a stepmother who didn't like him or his mild retardation, Harry turned to Frits for help. Frits and Bodil took in young Ken and for most of his childhood raised him as one of their own children.

Bodil with Bent, Ken Abel and Hans, about 1942

It was through Harry Beatty's collecting and the work of Dr. Roy Anduze in St. Thomas that the source of the terrible disease filariasis (known locally as elephantiasis) was finally identified and a cure developed by Ligget. Elephantiasis usually showed up in the legs as a massive swelling from hip to toe, sometimes in the arms. People who did laundry in the streams or who worked around wet banks were most liable to be affected. The cause turned out to be a worm that throve in wet soil conditions and entered the body usually through the feet. It could be transmitted by mosquito as well. Joe Bromstaff, Carl Lawaetz's chief vegetable gardener at Little La Grange suffered with this painful disease most of his life. Frits recalls hearing the story of one old man from the neighborhood who developed elephantiasis. His testicles got as large as coconuts. The man couldn't stand the pain, nor could he walk. He tried to castrate himself with a piece of glass, similar to the way one does a bull, but a man isn't made the same way and he nearly died of his self–imposed surgery. Still the man lived another ten or twelve years, all before Ligget developed the drug called Hetrazan between 1947 and 1951.

For entertainment for the Army Air Force troops and Marines in training at Benedict Field and also to keep his cowboys physically active, Frits liked arranging races and bull riding. Competition

Frits's famous race horse "Tommy Hawk" and jockey James McIntosh

with the other ranchers always drew a crowd. Because the original Betty's Hope Race Track was shut down, they made a track near Frederiksted where Markoe Elementary School now stands. Frits says, "The race track wasn't fenced in all the way around then, and we had to sometimes catch the bulls if they ran the wrong way." At one rodeo for the Fourth of July 1942, one bull threw a Marine, then turned and headed for the crowd. Frits says, "I was up on the judges' stand and saw I could help. I jumped down to the ground, and then I couldn't move." The pain from the fall must have knocked him out, because Frits, whose memory is incredibly infallible, doesn't recall who caught the bull.

The damage to his right leg was very serious. "The doctors thought I had damaged cartilage and put my leg in a cast. When the cast came off, my foot was black. The Navy doctors sent me to St. Thomas where some specialists were and they began running some painful tests." He still recalls the horror of having the inside of his tibia bone gouged for material to examine. The doctors began treating Frits for an infection in the bone. The effects of radiation treatment left deep burns on his inner thighs; he was unable to sit on a horse. While Frits was still there confined to bed, St. Thomas had a bone–jarring earthquake. The wall behind his bed fell down, but he couldn't move or get out of the way. Fortunately, the most he got was a dusting of plaster. On the down side, the injury put an end to his service in the Home Guard, as well as horseback riding. He walked on crutches for the next two years. Young Hans recalls the constant smell of mentholated ointment through those years, which he rubbed into Frits's knee each night.

Hans began school in the fall of 1943, attending St. Patrick's in Frederiksted. Each morning he and Normy Francis, who took care of Annaly's horses, would ride over to Jolly Hill where Hans caught the school bus into town. There was a whole village of people living on Estate Montpellier in those years, so the bus had plenty of children to pick up. At the end of the day, Normy would be there with Hans's pony to carry him home to Annaly and farm chores. Not long after Hans began school, one of Frits's kidneys began to act up and move out of place. The kidney damage was due to many years on horse back and the same kidney stone from two years before which had never passed. About the same time, he had a bad fall and hit the same spot on his bad leg. "I had to crawl on one leg and my arms to reach the truck and drive home." If there are people who see the cowboy's life as one of ease and glory, Frits knows first hand about one filled with pains. That too is the cowboy life.

He was sent to Rider Memorial Hospital in Humacao, Puerto Rico, in 1942 for treatment on the kidney. Doctors there also saw a lump on his urethra and said he needed to have surgery. "They had me in a room with a bed mate the nurses said had poisoned a girl. Whether he did or not, the man was raving delirious, and over the night he died. That was upsetting enough, but in the morning my friend Oliver Heyn came in and said he had a vision and that I shouldn't do the operation. Well that scared the devil out of me so I left." Frits went into San Juan to Presbyterian Hospital where another doctor determined the loose kidney was causing a kink in the urethra. "To keep the kidney from flopping around and causing such pain, the doctor tied it tightly to my lowest rib." Despite that treatment his system went into shock, and for the next two years some of his fingers were numb.

He may have been able to tolerate the numbness in his hand, but his left leg continued to act up intolerably. Naval doctors in St. Thomas diagnosed his problem as a giant cell tumor. Canaday insisted he come to Harkness Pavilion. In 1943, Frits received special permission to fly to Miami on a military transport and from there took a train up to New York City to see specialists at Canaday's request. Frits remembers the shock he felt at seeing "whites–only" drinking fountains and toilets along the train route through the southern states. He says there was no wonder in him anymore at why our men were so angry about the treatment they were getting in the south as soldiers.

Frits got to New York on crutches and stayed at the home of widow Crawford in New York City. He had an appointment to meet with Canaday, but, because of his war work, Canaday kept him waiting for over an hour. Canaday's daughter, Doreen, was there also waiting with her little boy, and she spent much time getting acquainted with Frits. When he was finally called in, Canaday had three phones ringing on his desk and could only spare him five minutes to discuss the leg. What Canaday had done, however, was get Frits the best bone specialist in the country, maybe in the world, a gentlemen about seventy–five years old, named Dr. Darah. Darah's former student and now assistant was Dr. Wilson, one of the two best black doctors in the U.S. and, in one of those amazing coincidences of life, a man who had been born at Estate River, St. Croix. "After a week of observation and testing, Dr. Wilson told me they had determined that I did not have cancer, and I was free to go. Well, it was time to pay, so I asked him how much? Dr. Wilson said, 'How much can you afford to pay?' I felt a cold sweat running down. Finally the doctor said fifty cents. I responded, 'Well Doctor, I had planned to pay forty cents so I will have to up it.' When I got home I sent him a hundred dollars. Wilson said he didn't need any money, but he did advise that if there was any further trouble the leg should be cut off."

Despite his relief about the cancer diagnosis being wrong, the thought of losing his leg if it gave him any further trouble was frightening. He couldn't imagine driving a car with one leg, Frits couldn't even imagine how he could walk. With two sons of his own, plus Ken, and his much loved wife, he didn't dare consider what would happen then.

During his time in New York, Frits visited with a lot of Crucians who had migrated to the city for work. Among them was Ashley Totten, head of the Sleeping Car Porters Union at the time, who "kept a little dinner" for Frits. It was a cold, wet, rainy night, he remembers, the first time he had been out on crutches in such weather. The taxi fellow was kind enough to walk him up to Totten's apartment to make sure he could make it.

A year after leaving New York cancer–free, Frits had to have a disk removed from his spine, another cowboy consequence. His back was opened up and then he was encased in a body cast. Recovery was awful; Frits said to his doctor, "You had the pleasure but I had the pain. The bill for that was a hundred dollars, but at the time I didn't have it. The doctor said, 'Don't worry, if you ever get lucky in a poker game, send me seventy–five dollars.'"

Frits's health worried the entire family, who also feared for the extensive Lawaetz and Tornoe families in embattled Europe. And the family worried about Far who was ailing. Eventually Far went over to St. Thomas to consult with Dr. Roy Anduze who was commissioner of health and a good friend as well. Surgery revealed he had an advanced case of prostate disease, for which there was no remedy. Frits spent many nights sitting up with his father until Anna returned home early in 1945 to help Mor care for him. Carl's eightieth birthday passed with little celebration. The news of Germany's surrender on 7 May, ending the war in Europe, must have eased Carl's mind a little. Carl died on 20 May 1945 and is buried on the grounds of Little La Grange, his own farm and dream of a lifetime.

— Chapter Twenty–One —

Bodil's Trip and Ralph George

Denmark had been occupied by Germany since 1940, and all of the Lawaetzes worried because Else's husband was Jewish, and they knew Jews were being rounded up. By war's end Bodil was frantic about her own family as well. Nothing was going to suit Bodil except to go over and see for herself, and she wanted to take her two boys. After school closed in the summer of 1946, Bodil, Hans, age ten, and Bent, eight, sailed to New York where people thought she was crazy to go to Europe when everyone there was trying to get out. While Bodil assailed the East Asiatic Company booking offices, the boys learned city stickball from their hosts in New York. They shared the two–bedroom apartment of an old friend who had two daughters. It was a sixth–floor walkup, Hans recalls, no elevator.

After weeks of hearing refusals, Bodil finally rode the train down to their main offices in Philadelphia. There the head of the company listened quietly to her pleas and then said her accent reminded him of a friend's wife named Tiny. Bodil asked if he was speaking of Tiny and Svend Mylner. Told yes, she explained that Tiny, who had been born a Paiewonsky, was her best friend from St. Thomas, and Svend had owned the River complex farm where Bodil lived when she first returned to St. Croix and married Frits. That link was all it took. Bodil got a letter to be given to the company people in New York, which directed them to give her the best first–class cabin on the next freighter out.

Bodil and the boys sailed to Denmark in great splendor on a thirty to fifty passenger freighter, where Bodil was joined by her sisters Annette and Nina and their children. They stayed first with Bodil's parents in a summer cottage in Hellebaek which is recorded

The Tornoe family. Back row (l–r): Annette, Nina, Bodil; middle row: Mr. Tornoe, Nina's daughter Miriam, Mrs. Tornoe; front row: Annette's son Graham, Nina's son Robin, and Bodil's boys Bent and Hans.

in a fine photo sent to Frits of the Tornoes with their three daughters, four grandsons and one granddaughter, all smiling. Hans recalls Denmark had many bombed out buildings, but he loved the cottage on the coast across from Sweden. His maternal grandfather took them all on long walks through the woods behind the cottage and along the rough, cold beaches of the North Sea. When autumn came Bodil's sisters returned to their homes in Bristol, England, and the Tornoes returned to Hellev to their retirement village housing. Bodil and the boys moved in with family friends who lived over a pottery factory just a few blocks away from her parents; it was quite close to Copenhagen.

The Lawaetzes spent the next six months of postwar hardship there. Hans and Bent couldn't attend school since they didn't speak Danish when they arrived, although they became proficient by the end of the ten months. Hans remembers staying with his Aunt Else a few times and attending dancing classes with his Lawaetz cousins, Merete and Otto. He said that it was a very cold winter; sledding and ice skating were his favorite activities.

Meanwhile, back in St. Croix changes were underway. Scattered about on all of the estates under Annaly Farms were many choices of homesites, but Ward M. Canaday liked the gentle manners of Bodil Lawaetz and found Estate Annaly much more suitable to entertaining the high–powered friends he was bringing down in order to encourage them to invest in St. Croix. Annaly greathouse had become so much of a showplace since Frits had taken over, that it was part of the scenic tours given at the time. While Bo was away, Ward Canaday had Annaly windmill converted into a charming apartment of four bedrooms and three baths and hired Ralph George of Grove Place as a full–time cook and butler. Prior to that time, Canaday had stayed at the River Estate house, with Maud as the cook, but found the site too small for entertaining.

By this time the Annaly Farm complex was a huge operation. Several key men were working to keep it all smoothly run. Oswald Bess who had come from Black Rock, Barbados at the age of twelve,

The converted mill at Annaly

was head cowboy at River, later followed by Eluterio "Lute" Bermudez. Lute's father "Aquelo" also worked for Annaly Farms and Lute's son Tonio would join the operation years later. Back in the 1940s, Marcelo Maldonado was foreman of the sugar operation. Joe Mills who drove a truck at River had been there since well before Canaday bought the operation, as had George Byron, Juan and Marco Ayala, all of whom worked with the cane, as well as James Bastian, a foreman and superior race horse trainer. Leonard Schrader ran the bulldozer at River up until the late 1950s, as did Joe Hodge. The extensive Guadeloupe family worked for Annaly as well, including Dan Dan, Gorilla, JJ and Gully. All of the Guadeloupes were ox cart men with a passionate dislike for tractors.

Don Daniel Correa was the head cowboy based at Mt. Victory. Bobo Gordon, a cane driver foreman at Annaly and later a hoist operator, lived at Oxford; James Heyliger had been overseer when Annaly was bought by Canaday and served in that post until his retirement in 1950. Erik Lawaetz was manager at River; he started there in 1940 after Frits moved to Annaly and stayed on until 1950. He had married his sweetheart Jenny Christensen and all three of their children learned to walk at River: Roy, Mona and David. Hans would follow in his family footsteps and also live at River where his daughter Jodie was born. Years later the youngest of Frits's boys, Fritsie, lived there and the youngest of Frits's grandchildren, Jens, was born there. The house at River has been as much "home" to the Lawaetz family as Little La Grange.

Into this continuity of families and farm work, Canaday had been encouraging his friends in the states to come down and invest, either in Puerto Rico or the Virgin Islands, since the early 1930s. With persistence and enthusiasm, he personally was responsible for bringing down fifty–six millionaires and even captured the attention of presidents. Franklin Roosevelt had come to St. Croix on 8 July 1934, and Canaday invited his friend, President Harry Truman, to do so as well. Many prominent Americans did come and take up residence including the architect William G. Thayer, Jr., and his wife, Marion, who bought Butler Bay; George and Georgia Burnett of Boston bought an old town house in Christiansted; Ward's friend Howard Wall invested in Cane Garden and began competing with him in cattle. Canaday found much local enthusiasm for reclaiming the historic structures and joined with Attorney R.H. Amphlett Leader, the Armstrongs and Skeoches, as well as Pearl Byrd Larsen, Dick and Tina Richards, the van Ripers and dozens of others who finally formed the St. Croix Landmarks League. Canaday was a founding member of the St. Croix Museum established by the St. Croix Municipal Council in 1951 to spearhead the collection and display of local artifacts. His financial support was given very privately.

Much of the responsibility for Ward's entertainment success fell on the shoulders of Ralph George, a serene, self–contained gentleman, first hired in 1947. Ralph George was born at Two Friends on St. Croix on 13 March 1919. He says he is a "land crab," having never left the island, even by boat. Ralph attended St.

Patrick's through sixth grade; then, lacking the cost of real shoes — not ones made from old tires, he had to stop going. In 1938 Ralph joined the Civilian Conservation Corps (CCC). The corps, a New Deal unemployment relief project specializing in forestry programs in the Virgin Islands, was run by military men at first: Mr. McGuire, Charles Gray and then Mr. Lantz. The first civilian head of the corps was Larry Merrill from Maine, a forester and a bachelor. Merrill stayed on in St. Croix and married Tova Farber, born at Butler Bay, and through Tova became the owner of the Christiansted Apothecary Hall.

When Ralph first began work in the corps' camp, located where the old Rasmussen market was until the 1960s in Grande Princesse, he was put in the kitchens and began as a mess boy, cutting vegetables and cleaning pots. He recalls that, in the old days prior to 1949, the east–end terrain beyond what is now the Buccaneer Hotel was undeveloped with wild animals like deer and pigs. Mr. Pentheny, who owned much of the land, had a contract to provide meats to the CCC. Ralph George remembered that the camp was bringing in two cooks in rotation from St. Thomas who stayed for a month each. None of the Crucian men were allowed to be cooks. When Merrill came, he said, "Nonsense, teach the Crucians how to cook and cut out the cost of bringing those other men over." Ralph's first cooking job was baking bread. He liked the camp; he got paid four dollars a month while his mother got eight dollars a month; he was

The two Annaly cooks: Ralph George and Teresa Napoleon Clarke

provided with all of his clothes, meals, and housing, and had his weekends free.

In 1942 the camp was closed. Ralph moved to Grove Place and went to work for the Benedict Field quartermaster, and then worked in the mess hall where he learned American cooking. Ralph recalls that on the base most foods were canned or dried, they only got fresh local foods just once a week. Ralph knew the Lawaetz boys from childhood, they were neighbors; and now he often saw Bodil and Erik, also working at Benedict Field. The air base mess hall was located on the north side of the hill which is the north border of today's runway, and one entered by way of the posts just north of the Evans highway on the east airport road. It made for interesting cooking, Ralph remembers, because the Sixty–fifth Infantry was composed mainly of Puerto Rican soldiers while the Air Force personnel were all continentals, and neither liked the other's idea of good cooking. Ralph first met Ward Canaday when he served as waiter at a government event. Canaday liked his quiet, self–assured style, found out he could cook as well and, as the mill house neared completion in 1947, promptly hired him for Annaly. For many happy years Ralph commuted from Grove Place to Annaly on his horse, Marie.

Mariam Canaday did not like to travel by airplane so she came for a six–week visit by ship in order to be hostess for President Truman's visit on 23 February 1948. A lot of effort went into decorating the place up very well, Ralph remembered. A temporary roof was put on the upper terrace at the mill, because at that time of year there was always a chance of rain. Frits recalls that, "Mrs. Canaday had a sharp, sarcastic wit and little affection for the president who was a close friend of her husband's. When Mr. Truman was taken up to see the view from the top of the mill she slyly suggested a little push over the wall might be good for the country! The luncheon for eighty persons, seated, was successful and Wesley Thomas's band was a big hit." Truman returned to his ship, the USS *Williamsburg*, for the night amid heavy security. Ralph said: "The day after the party Mr. Truman sailed off for

President Truman, in grey suit (front, second from left), walking away from Annaly mill; Jeep at lower right

Guantanamo Bay and a terrific storm came and tore our temporary shelter apart."

Ralph remembered that Mr. Canaday was on Capitol Hill on 1 March 1954, the day several Puerto Ricans shot five congressmen during a congressional session. Canaday was there testifying before members of a tax committee and, as usual, greeted the security guards on duty. One of the guards he knew was injured in the shooting, and Canaday offered the use of his mill for recovery. Mr. Merriman and his wife came for two weeks. He was quite ill, Ralph recalls, and his medication dyed the sheets. Ralph said Mr. Canaday did a lot of nice things for people and never claimed or wanted credit for them. When guests came to use the mill, Frits and Bodil would join them the first night for dinner, to advise them of interesting places, and see them again for dinner the last night.

Ralph provided all the meals and cleaning and brought in a washing woman if ladies stayed.

In the early years, Mr. Canaday held a lot of parties at Annaly for important political movers and shakers, Frits said. "He was the American co–chairman of the Caribbean Commission, a little United Nations type of effort by the American government. Some of his decisions were very last minute, like the evening he returned home from a meeting at the Buccaneer with me and suggested, at 1:00 in the morning, that we have a party that evening, because it would be his last chance before leaving."

Canaday was the boss so Frits arranged to have a four hundred pound bull shot at 5:00 A.M., then hauled it over to Miss Gena Samuel in order to have it roasted in an old Crucian oven and ready by 7:00 that night. "Bodil and Ralph George took care of the decorating and cleaning and pulling the rest of the dinner together. Ideally the meat should have been seasoned overnight, but there was not time for it," Frits recalls. Ralph rounded up twelve to fifteen boys to serve as waiters, and old Mr. Messer went around and collected the members of his string band, including Simmonds with the kerosene pan. Frits had Jenny Thurland make calls through the central exchange, and, even though it was at the last minute, three hundred people came for cocktails and dinner and had a good party.

Frits says Mr. Canaday never remembered who he invited, so for preparations they always had to increase the number of expected guests. "Then it was a problem because everyone wanted to be included, so we changed over to smaller parties for a dozen people or so. The biggest party was for John Snyder, secretary of the Department of the Treasury under President Truman, and his wife, Mary. He was here to rest and it was a big bit of trouble trying to keep the press away from him. Then after three days they felt up to a little socializing so we had a party." Al Hayes, who worked as manager at the Buccaneer Hotel in the early 1950s and eventually owned a General Motors car dealership on St. Croix, recalls meeting Canaday and being impressed by his solid gold cufflinks shaped like Jeeps. Canaday told him that only three pairs were made. He had given one set to Roosevelt, another to Stalin and kept the last set for himself, a memento of the incredible number of jeeps sold during World War II to the Allied partners. Canaday, who had just one daughter, bequeathed his cufflinks to Frits.

Ward Canaday on steps of Annaly mill

— Chapter Twenty–Two —

Conservation and the Nelthropp Legacy

In 1946, Ward Canaday bought the River–Fountain complex, east of Annaly, which included Fountain, Parasol, Solitude, Mt. Eagle, Hermitage, Blue Mountain, Prosperity and River estates. This brought his total ownership up to 4,200 acres, the largest private holding ever amassed in the territory. The estates under Annaly, his first purchase, included Mt. Victory, Pleasant Vale, Rose Hill, Oxford, Mt. Stewart, Wills Bay, Bodkin and Sweet Bottom. Lands he leased across the northwest end of the island until the 1970s brought the number up to 5,900 acres out of a total of nearly 54,000 on St. Croix. Frits managed a total of twenty–seven owned and leased estates that supported 1,500 head of cattle and 300 acres in sugar cane. Frits spent all of his time working from a Jeep now, rather than from the back of a horse, a lot less damaging to his body.

Some of the cattle at Annaly Farms came from stock originally bred by Bromley Nelthropp, who used to tend his herd in the manner of old Carl Lawaetz: on horseback in starched white linen shirt and pants with a white bush hunter's hat. Nelthropp's cattle, N'Dama from Senegal, West Africa, which had been mixed with Red Poll from England by way of Trinidad, were so tame they wouldn't be chased on horseback, but could be driven into the pens by a cowboy on foot. This was the stock Frits wanted to work with, but Canaday was still experimenting, and in 1947 he had twenty–five cattle shipped in from the King Ranch in Texas, eight of which were bulls. Hans remembers there were four bulls for Annaly Farms, one for Selwyn Fleming and one for Norman Skeoch. He couldn't recall who got the last two. Betty Skeoch recalled that her husband Norman had been restricted by the King Ranch in 1939 to buying just one bull and two heifers, and how glad he was when Ward sent another bull down for him.

Hans remembers it as a bad experience, the cattle, three–quarters Santa Gertrudis, were "wild as hell and had never seen a fence line. At the time we were raising about 1,500 N'Dama crosses." The Texas cattle did not adapt to tropical conditions, nor were they resistant to ticks so they had to be dipped every two weeks. One time a calf got bawling and the mother came charging, and Frits had to dive into the dip pit to avoid being gored. Despite three or four scourings to rid his skin of the arsenic, Frits's skin peeled several layers deep and it was quite painful, he remembers. The cowboys, Frits included, disliked the new temperamental cattle so much the crew gave them bad names in Spanish. Canaday accepted the judgment and agreed to invest in the Nelthropp Senegalese mix which went back a long way.

Nelthropp's family originally came to St. Croix as farmers in the nineteenth century and settled mid–island on St. Croix. The Senegalese cattle which they raised were small but highly tolerant of both heat and drought conditions; on the down side the meat was tough and milk production was just adequate. Nelthropp started some crosses, but early Zebu imports did not work out well. Around 1880 George Elliott of Estate Longford imported sixty N'Dama from Senegal, West Africa (locally called Senegalese), four of which were bulls. Several were made available to the Nelthropps and were put at the farm in Estate Granard. They proved to be very gentle but, being horned, sometimes injured themselves and their handlers. Long–horned oxen were favored for field work; for milkers and meat production, horns were not desirable. By the end of the century, young Bromley Nelthropp wanted his stock to produce more milk and beef. Bromley thought he could breed for productivity and gentility as well. Among his searches he went to Trinidad in 1914, where the British experimental station there was willing to part with a Red Poll (hornless) bull named Captain Kidd. Captain Kidd had been sent over from England but the farmers, wanting horned oxen, left Kidd unloved. Bromley maintained he spent two thousand dollars for it, in an era when twenty dollars or so was generally the going price for a cow. At whatever price, Nelthropp returned with Captain Kidd and put it to breed with Senegalese cattle at the family's Estate Boetzberg. According to a *St. Croix Avis* editorial by Bruce Millar in January 1953, Bromley mixed in a little Red Devon and Zebu and kept crossing Red Polls back in, until finally he settled on seven characteristics: all red color, high milk production, good conformation, fertility, heat tolerance, no sign of horns, and gentle dispositions. Cattle failing to meet these standards were sent to slaughter. There were many suspicions that not all were slaughtered, and that in the dark of night neighbors were wont to introduce their female cattle into the bull pasture for a little free crossing, but those incidents happened later on when the breeding results began to be appreciated.

Frits was well acquainted with Nelthropp's herd; his father had invested in them in 1919 and the family had been very satisfied with them. The Nelthropps and Lawaetzes were close friends over many decades, visiting back and forth between estates, talking cattle, and playing poker after dining together. As old Bromley came near the end of his days, there were bidders for Bromley's herd from many parts of the Caribbean but friendship held. He agreed to sell the herd to Annaly Farms. In March 1949, Canaday purchased 129 of 132 cattle, the rest going to Nelthropp's nephews, Ceddie and Henry. It was in this year, 1949, that Frits began his breeding program with the Nelthropp herd and also inaugurated the more detailed records on what would be called Senepol cattle, the first true American cattle breed.

Cowboys spent many hours in the corrals ear tagging and branding the new cattle with Annaly's "WC" mark. Then just one bull was placed with a herd of twenty–five heifers and cows, harem–style. As each calf was born it was ear tagged, weighed and re–weighed twice a year. Weaning weights were adjusted to reflect a uniform 205 days. At the age of six months, new calves were branded with their ear tag numbers. As the calves matured, any that did not met Frits's standards were culled and sold to slaughter. The best of the best were bred again.

Frits was the expert on proper island conservation and irrigation methods and what private capital could do to improve farming practices. From observation and experience, he also knew what was working and what was not in the federal programs on St. Croix. As the general manager of Canaday's operation, he testified in 1948 before a visiting panel from the U.S. Department of Interior about the cultivation of sugar cane by private enterprise during the past twenty years. He noted that private interest in cane cultivation had decreased considerably due to three key factors: lowering of the water table caused by decreased hillside cultivation, congressionally mandated increases in the cost of labor and materials without an increase in the price of sugar, and lack of technical advice.

Frits told the panel that "formerly hillsides were cultivated with cane banks which retained the water, but presently they are overgrazed as pasture which led to compacting of the soil, and run–off. During the rainy seasons the coastlines are flooded with mud instead of the rain seeping slowly through the hills into the acquefers."

Frits told them that "in 1937, the price was $3.70 a ton of cane; straight labor was paid at 70 cents a day. Job labor paid 35 cents per ton for cutting and 25 cents per ton for loading and hauling. The 1948 crop, the price was $7.10 per ton, straight labor is now $2.00 per day, cutting is now $1.10 per ton and loading and hauling is getting 75 cents per ton. For the above figures you will find that we are today paying about 300% more for labor and only receiving 100% more for our product. In addition to this, materials and supplies have also gone up about 300%."

He also told them that St. Croix was in a time warp, while

elsewhere in the world methods of cultivation had improved. He blamed the lack of an active agricultural station for the information gap. He pointed out that USDA staff members in Rio Piedras, Puerto Rico, had two days during a four–day convention to show films and discuss experiments, herbicides, cane varieties, application and cultivation methods, insect control and other specialties to farmers. "That is the type of technical aid St. Croix needs," Frits said, "It is impossible to obtain same from our local station, due to its being under the Department of the Interior and the resulting low appropriations." He reminded them that formerly St. Croix had an active experimental station under the Department of Agriculture which created the St. Croix "12–4" variety, for many years a leading cane in the entire Caribbean. Frits spoke also about the need for tools to assist the small growers, and the necessity for them to be available at the right time. The hearings resulted in the closing of the Virgin Islands Company (VICO) by Interior. A new federal company was created the following year to mend the problems Frits and others had so eloquently detailed. It would be known as the Virgin Islands Corporation (VICORP).

Four of the five supervisors of the St. Croix Soil Conservation District in 1952 (L–R): Henry Schuster, I. Gatewood James; Frits Lawaetz, president; and Henry Nelthropp, secretary

— Chapter Twenty–Three —

The First Registered American Cattle Breed

The federal government's programs and funding might be inept and frustrating, but Frits, Lute Bermudez, his cattle foreman, and Marcelo Maldonado, the sugar foreman at River, ran Annaly Farms like a finely tuned clock. It was around this time that they stopped harvesting cane at Annaly, because the River Estates were better for planting. Bodil was home and happy again. She had accepted the task of keeping rainfall records for the National Weather Bureau in 1947 after her return and was happy for things to occupy her time. Hans and Bent were gone most of the day, excellent students attending St. Patrick's Catholic School in Frederiksted. Frits tried to attend every ball game the boys played.

Soon after the family celebrated Bent's tenth birthday on 22 February 1949 they learned Bodil was once again pregnant, and they were both shocked and delighted. A lusty boy was born bawling on 4 September 1949; he was christened as Frits Tornoe but was ever after called Fritsie. Since the new mother and infant were given the very same room in the Frederiksted hospital that Bodil had used after the birth of her two older boys, Frits was on the alert for mice. But Frits said that young Fritsie made such a noise all the time, he kept them scared away!

Active and curious, Fritsie became everyones' pet. He learned cleaning and cooking at Ralph George's knee during the day and listened to his father's stories about the cattle at night. When a stranger once asked the two–year old who his father was, Fritsie responded quite seriously that he had two fathers, a white one called Daddy and a black one called Ralph. And he was right, for those were the men who were raising him. By the time he was three, Fritsie rode nearly every day in the Jeep with his dad or on horseback with Wyson on the rounds of the pastures, checking fence lines and conditions of the fields, learning firsthand all the jobs that came with raising cane and cattle, as his father and brothers had done before him.

In 1951, thanks to the enthusiasm of the Lawaetz males for sports, Annaly Farms became the sponsor of a baseball team called the Annaly Athletics, hiring O'Neal Sackey as coach. Hans played on the Athletics team for four years. Frits is rightly proud of that team, for three of its players went on to play professionally in stateside major leagues: Joe Christopher, first to the Pittsburgh Pirates then to the New York Mets; Elmo Plaskett, to Pittsburgh as a catcher; and Julio Navarro, as a pitcher for the Detroit Tigers. Another player, Cinque Soto, made it to the minor leagues. That was quite an accomplishment for an island of just thirteen thousand people.

(L–R) Bent, Hans, Fritsie, circa 1951

About this time, Canaday had written to

Jaime Benitez requesting assistance in making breeding plans for Canaday's cattle. Benitez recommended Dr. C. Gaztambide Arrillago, the extension dairyman out of the University of Puerto Rico in Rio Piedras. Gaztambide wrote Frits that he wanted to meet Bromley Nelthropp and learn what breeding plans he had been using first; however Nelthropp had died the previous year. Gaztambide wrote Frits on 26 March 1951 that he had outlined a tentative breeding plan which he planned to discuss with Frits, "after he had studied the complete situation." He wrote further, "Then we will submit it to Mr. Canaday for approval. You realize this is a ten– to thirty–year program which requires a practical man at the wheel. I believe you can execute it, with the support of Mr. Canaday, and my advise [*sic*]."

On 10 April Gaztambide wrote Canaday saying he was authorized to go to St. Croix, and he sent Frits a sketch of points and a tentative breeding plan. He apparently did go between 8 and 10 May and found he was hardly needed. Gaztambide's conclusions were received by Mr. Canaday in Toledo on 14 June 1951 and his ten– to thirty–year program was out the window. Frits had been following an enviable plan himself, and Gaztambide had to admit they were just two or three generations away from imposing Senepol characteristics on the whole herd, in just six to nine years. There was nothing in the specialist's original recommendations of points and plans that Frits hadn't already instituted. In fact although Gaztambide originally recommended the Santa Gertrudis for adding more beefiness, he said the good type and prepotency of the Senepol breed makes the elimination of all other bulls of other breeds, except the Santa Gertrudis, advisable. He then recommended in the same letter that it would be better to import one or two more Red Poll bulls and not use the Gertrudis at all, because it is a three–way cross and too newly established (in 1940). All of these points had been made for years by Frits himself.

Frits and Dr. Gaztambide did select the best of the breed during his visit and recommended Canaday invest in one of Mr. Messer's bulls, which came from the original Nelthropp herd and possessed the scale and type being sought. Dr. Gaztambide wrote, "....the Senepol seems to be the best breed for the insular tropical climate, and possibly to continental climates....from the breeding viewpoint, there is no place for other breeds in the commercial herd....This new breed could have great economic and social significance for tropical countries and tropical people from the point of view of the beef supply...a very desirable goal. Thus in a general way, the establishment of the Senepol breed is not only an attractive possibility from the breeder's standpoint but also a business proposition worth serious consideration."

His colleagues concurred. Dr. Richard M. Bond, a regional biologist for the USDA Soil Conservation Service out of Oregon wrote on 3 July 1951, following a visit, "I was however, very much impressed by the breed developed on the island....most of these animals are under the management of Mr. Frits Lawaetz who is doing, I think, an extraordinary job of selection and breeding and I suspect that the confirmation of the breed can be improved rather rapidly without bringing in anything from outside." In fact, Dr. Bond was recommending to his friend, Howard Wall of Cane Garden, that he increase his herd of this type as fast as possible. Wall's success in calving with mixed breeds was close to seventy percent while Frits's Senepol calving was running about eighty–five percent successful.

Dr. Bond reported that Frits fed cottonseed meal and molasses to his herd, and they continued to make gains during a very long dry season. Supplemental feeding during the dry season, Dr. Bond wrote, was expected to take one–third off the time required to get an animal to suitable size for slaughter and should at least double the year–round capacity of the pastures. Bond also recommended that Howard Wall follow the practices imposed by Frits about keeping bulls away until the heifers were two years old, and selectively breeding for birth during growing seasons, as well as mowing and fertilizing the pastures themselves. So the experts came and learned, and Frits's system was the one adopted for all to follow.

About this time, Frits again felt uneasy about his health and ended up with an emergency appendectomy on 12 July 1951. He was back in the Jeep a week later.

Dr. Gaztambide suggested Frits invite Dr. A.E. Bowman in to see his herd. Bowman was the extension director emeritus of the U.S. Southern Region, having formerly served in Puerto Rico between 1936 and 1937, and for thirty–eight years as director out of Wyoming. Bowman had been invited by United States Secretary of Agriculture Charles Brannon to go to Puerto Rico and give talks. Frits became friendly with them all. They were even more grateful when the need arose for tetanus antitoxin in San Juan and Frits asked Canaday to arrange that. Ligget Pharmaceutical sent 150 vials, all paid for by Ward Canaday.

By June 1954 Dr. Gaztambide was writing about the choice of color for the trademark sign, suggesting cherry red because it was the closest to the breed. He also suggested calling them "Brahman," but Frits rejected that in favor of Senepol, which reflected their true and direct descent from the Red Poll and the Senegalese branches of the family. The cattle breed "Senepol" was recognized and registered as #593,722 on 29 December 1952 at the same time the name was trade marked. After all their hard work, it was a time of great personal pride for Frits and his men. It was a singular honor for Frits, now forty–five years old, to be acclaimed as the developer

Senepol calf and mother, #7115, true to the breed

with Ward Canaday of the first cross stock breed in the Caribbean and the first for the tropical climate in the Americas. The Senepol breed would eventually be registered and the name trade marked four times, including a Commercial Class 1 rating in August 1954, #643,420 for Saint Croix Senepol and, out of Puerto Rico, #8678 for Senepol and #9405 for Saint Croix Senepol.

The Senepol breed's distinguishing characteristics include: excellent milk and beef production, low birth weight, and tolerance of both heat and drought conditions. The Senepol is a solid dark mahogany brown, hornless, generally standing about five feet tall at the shoulder. The average weight of a cow is 1,100 pounds; a bull runs 1,800 to 2,000 pounds.

Cattle are carefully inspected quarterly and rated A, B, or C on each of several measurements and characteristics: height, weight, "confirmation" (evenly conformed muscles), and on other physical qualities. Based on these quarterly ratings, some cattle will be culled. Cattle with the highest ratings are kept for breeding. Those culled are slaughtered for beef.

The cattle are officially weighed at weaning and again two months later. "And then," Frits says, "trouble begins. The cattle youngster isn't much different from a human little boy or girl — they have to learn what not to put in their mouths. Generally this is learned in the pasture by paying attention to what the cows eat, but those little ones get into all sorts of things, and some are deadly; we've had cows die from eating mangoes, choking on the pits, a terrible loss, terrible way to die. And there are also some bushes that grow in the fields that will harm the cattle, if you are not careful. Those have to be kept out, dug up by hand before the cows get turned into the pasture."

Frits has always been very strict about careful grazing, and when the weather seemed to be turning towards a drought, he culled his herds rather than overgraze the lands. By 1950 he was managing a crew of ten. The range was separated into four districts for management purposes, with a foreman and helper in charge of each district. When extra hands were needed, Frits established a practice of hiring them from the trustee system at the jail. He maintains strong ties as well as personal friendships with island cattlemen specializing in Senepol: Oscar Henry at La Grange, the Nelthropp brothers at Granard south of Christiansted, and the Walls at Cane Garden southwest of Granard. Because of the complex system of branding the herds, it is considered impossible for one to be stolen and not identifiable.

Herding Senepol at Annaly in 1950 (L–R): Hans, Frits and Bent

Part III
The Legislative Years

— CHAPTER TWENTY–FOUR —

Politics: Personal, Universal and Intense

To understand why Frits did not rest on his laurels with a recognized cattle breed, or put more time into his family life, with his youngest son still not old enough for school, one has to know that Virgin Islanders' interest in politics in the 1950s was personal, universal and intense. With the exception of the Social Security System, established in 1935, there were few social programs or job guarantees. Islanders continued to look out for each other's interests through the extended family network and political action. Prior to 1936, voting rights were limited to less than six percent of the entire population because of income, sex and property requirements. University of the Virgin Islands history professor, Isaac Dookhan, noted in his book, *A History of the Virgin Islands of the United States*, that the colonial councils created by the U.S. Congress on 3 March 1917 "were severely limited in control over taxation, and they could not override the governor's legislative veto." The U.S. continued the two Danish districts: (1) St. Croix and (2) St. Thomas–St. John and all of their adjacent cays (islands). When Congress gave Virgin Islands males universal suffrage in 1935, females had to take their case to courts in both districts in order to vote.

Mindful of their history, voters in the 1950s were still fiercely protective of their hard won rights and flexed political muscle in constant challenge to the dictates of appointed government officials. Dookhan wrote that the dissatisfied voters wanted much more political power. He said, "the two objectives were by no means complementary: the unfranchised wanted the power to vote for men who could cater to their interest; the [national government and colonial council] representatives had no intention of sharing their political power if it might lead to the adoption of measures inimical to their interest" (Dookhan 276). St. Croix, with its primary activity in farming, had more to gain from political change; it had little in common with St. Thomas which focused on seaport trading. St. Thomians dominated the joint council meetings through alliances, while Crucians still resented the removal of the capital to Charlotte Amalie in 1871.

Under the Organic Act of 1936, the colonial councils were renamed municipal councils. Additionally, the territory was no longer under military rule; new governors were appointed by the United States president and confirmed by Congress. While some of the civilian governors chosen were purely political appointees, many of them were talented administrators. They also were savvy political people who made certain, as had their predecessors, they aligned themselves with the power elite: property owners and those with large financial interests in the islands, etc. But people of modest means, long ignored, wanted control over their lives and they wanted it *NOW*, so the experiences of all of the appointed civilian governors were constantly fractious. Municipal council members mostly divided themselves along the sides of labor and management and, by those sides, either supported or opposed the activities and budget proposals of the governors. St. Croix members were more likely to support the governor's actions, St. Thomas members more often aligned with labor. Frits's personal position on this matter was that strength comes from financial stability, which demonstrates that you can run your own government. Power comes from that financial strength; it does not precede it.

One particular bone of contention about the civilian governors irritated nearly everyone: they were all outsiders. Islanders believed they had talented local leaders and wanted natives appointed to the highest position in their territory. American politicians eventually did make some efforts to appoint persons they expected would have something in common with Virgin Islanders: President Truman named a black federal judge with island experience, William H. Hastie, as governor, who served from 1946 to 1950. Truman then appointed the first local man, Morris DeCastro, who served as governor from 24 March 1950 until April 1954. President Eisenhower canceled that popular advance when he named a black engineer from Iowa, Archie Alexander, as governor. What the Republicans and Eisenhower did not comprehend, did not even notice, was that, while islanders were not color conscious, they were quite conscious of status and class. Besides taking a step backwards from local leaders, naming as governor an untrained political supporter was seen by many as a slap in the face.

The time was ripe for change. Following the end of World War II, candidates for the municipal councils were younger men, veterans, eager for action. They were not alone. Islanders who had earlier migrated to New York City and Washington D.C., rising to positions of power in politics there, stood up early on behalf of greater autonomy for islanders, not incidentally advancing their own political power base as well. The route to national power brokering lay, not in "chumming up" to appointed governors, but in wielding influence with cabinet members and members of Congress in Washington. To do that, one needed the political party connections; the New York–based "Virgin Islanders in Exile" group had that clout, as did the "V.I. Congressional Council," formed and headed by Caspar Holstein since 1923. Virgin Islands council members were their willing partners in assaults on the "hallowed halls" in Washington.

Governor Archie Alexander was sworn in on 9 April 1954. With the help of Charles Claunch, his second–in–command and an experienced Washington power broker, Alexander worked with Senator Butler and Congressman Miller, both Republicans from Nebraska, to amend the Organic Act of 1936 to give him the superior powers he thought Eisenhower intended him to have as governor of the territory. Local opponents, through Earle Ottley's Unity party newspaper, the *Photo News,* declared that Alexander, Butler, Miller and Tony Lausi, director of territories in the Department of Interior, were conspiring "in malice and dedicated to the acknowledged task of putting 'uppity' Virgin Islanders in their places." There were many in the islands who disagreed; Ottley called them a "tiny minority motivated by greed or racial bias." In fact they were men like Ottley's usual political ally Walter I.M. Hodge, councilman of St. Croix, who went to Washington personally to testify in favor of the Butler bill. St. Thomian political power broker Ralph Paiewonsky liked it as well. Other St. Croix council members, namely Ann Abramson, Eric Carroll and Raymond Pedro, also urged passage. All were people who often had been allied with Ottley, but on this issue they simply had a sharp difference of opinion with members of the newly born Unity party. Because divided opinions had stalled it for many years, revision of the organic act was not expected to pass any time soon.

Notwithstanding expectations, little more than two and a half months after Alexander took over as governor, the Revised Organic Act passed in Congress on 22 June 1954. Candidates had little more than three months to get ready to campaign for one of the eleven seats in the new Legislature of the Virgin Islands. Certain members of the now disbanded municipal councils vowed to take control of the legislature and make Alexander's life miserable.

— CHAPTER TWENTY–FIVE —

1954: A Run for Office

Frits watched political activities very carefully, both nationally and locally, because they directly affected the well–being of farming on St. Croix. Minimum wages, shipping regulations, taxes and programs within the U.S. Department of Agriculture affecting the Virgin Islands depended on political clout in Congress. A host of locally legislated activities also affected the profit and loss columns. Frits took the brunt of the worry for Annaly Farms, because it was his responsibility to make the cattle farming operation profitable. Maintaining good relations with responsible leaders in Washington was imperative. He was not happy with what he saw taking place on the political scene.

Frits's social and political conscience had been honed by his family, solid Lutheran farmers and ministers; Frits lived comfortably with honesty, justice, temperance, prudence, courage and honor. His ancestors also had served in government positions: his adoptive grandfather, Otto, helped form social programs in the Folkting (Danish parliament); his father, Carl, had been nominated to both the Danish colonial council and American colonial council as a representative of the people who had no voting rights until 1934.

Frits began public service in 1946 as a member of the federally created Virgin Islands Soil and Water Conservation Board. As part of that work, and as a farmer in his own right, Frits testified before government committees locally and nationally, and wrote letters

Frits's father, Carl Lawaetz, was a member of the colonial councils. In the picture above, Carl, at right, has his back to the camera.

with his concerns to Washington. During his tenure as chairman, Frits played a major part in getting the earth dam program started with federal grants, working with Senator Butler and Congressman Jensen, each of whom chaired the Interior Committee in their respective house of Congress. Frits had taken them to see earth dams, one at Diamond, built by Gordon Skeoch, the other at Upper Love, built by Erik Lawaetz. Butler and Jensen arranged for federal grants to be appropriated over many years for the earth dam and watershed program to help raise water tables in both districts, supplying good water for people, cattle and plants.

As the first legislative campaign in the Virgin Islands began to take shape over the summer of 1954, Frits was uneasy with the prospect of no longer being able to go down the street and tell his councilman how he felt about a bill because, under the Revised Organic Act of 1954, half of those voting on St. Croix issues could be from St. Thomas or St. John. The attacks on Butler who had proved himself a friend to the islands did not sit well either.

Early in October, a well–respected attorney and acknowledged leader in the St. Croix community named R.H. Amphlett Leader called Frits at Annaly and asked if he might bring a guest up for lunch. Frits easily agreed, for Bodil was a renowned hostess. When Attorney Leader arrived on 3 October his guest was the highly respected labor hero Charles Ruebel. Charles Ruebel was an old man at this time, running a newspaper for Virgin Islanders in New York City and supporting islanders' causes before Congress. But Frits knew him as one of the important labor leaders who began to fight for workers rights in the early decades of the century. Reubel had begun a night school for laborers in Christiansted back in 1913 with David Hamilton Jackson, Sammy Crowe and Colonel Crowe, at a time when most boys left school for work by the age of twelve. After David Hamilton Jackson went to Denmark and met with the king, Ruebel, Jackson and James Bough were part of a group that formed and ran the *Herald* when the king of Denmark approved a free newspaper in 1915.

After lunch, both Ruebel and Attorney Leader spoke eloquently about the Lawaetz family's long contribution to fair pay and fair working conditions for their workers at Jolly Hill and Little La Grange, and their good care of the village houses. Then Attorney Leader made their case clear.

"Mr. Lawaetz, are you pleased with the candidates that are going to St. Thomas to represent you?" Amphlett asked.

Frits was forced to respond with honesty: "No...."

With that confession on the table, Ruebel and Leader wasted no time in convincing Frits that his duty lay, as it had with his father before him, in giving his time to public service for the betterment of his community. Reflecting on their concerns and his own, Frits had four days to think about it before the filing deadline on 7 October.

Frits talked the possibility through with Bodil. Both Hans and Bent were away at Westtown School, a Quaker boarding school in Pennsylvania, Bent leaving for the first time that September. Little Fritsie, just past five years old, was not taking so much of Bodil's time. Already keeping all the records and correspondence as secretary of Annaly Farms, Bodil thought that carrying a bit more of the work during the sixty–day sessions seemed possible, and she encouraged Frits to try. On 7 October he picked up his application for nomination. The first person to sign was David McBean, next his good friend policeman James Bennerson, then Mr. Gardine signed, followed by Maximo Garcia and Ed Mullgrav. "By lunch time I had all the signatures I needed." At the age of forty–seven, he jumped wholeheartedly into the political fray which would last, in all, for more than twenty–four years.

Frits decided to run as an independent for a district seat, one of two up for election. (The new legislature would also include six at large senators and two from the St. Thomas–St. John district). He asked Eddie Hendricks to serve as his first campaign manager and to help him make a plan. Antoine Joseph volunteered to get Frits prepared. Frits asked his friend Julio Delgado to fix up loudspeaker systems which got plugged into light poles at each stop, and he began drafting his first political speech. Frits recalls that, "I prayed to God to give me wisdom and courage to say what I wanted to say."

The *West End News* covered his first engagement on 17 October at the Frederiksted bandstand, and Frits thought he pulled a big crowd. He urged his listeners to "send strong men to look out for the interest of St. Croix, otherwise we will be annexed to St. Thomas like Buck Island is to St. Croix. I got a big clapping," he remembers. Old Alexander Moorhead came over and complemented him, saying, "You surprised us all."

Frits was pitting himself as a novice against four former legislators and two Puerto Ricans whom political pundits were sure would carry the Hispanic votes. Frits took to stumping for votes like a professional campaigner. Back in those days, the manner of campaigning was to send a person in advance with the message for the neighborhood people and to put a little notice in the newspaper that a certain candidate would speak in their area at a set time. Unlike anyone else running, Frits had five hundred copies of his speech printed in Spanish and English to hand out after each talk. His first ad was small, titled "Campaign Meeting, Voters and the General Public Cordially Invited." He spoke over radio station

WIVI, in English and Spanish, on Thursday, 21 October at 6:30 P.M. He spoke at Marley Center the same night at 8:30 P.M. On 24 October, he was in Correa's estate Baron's Spot, and at 8:00 P.M. on 28 October he visited Fredensborg. He spoke at Christiansted bandstand at 8:30 P.M. on the twenty–ninth and was happy with his reception. He was back in Frederiksted at 5:00 P.M. on 31 October and finished the evening in Grove Place at 7:00 P.M. He was welcomed everywhere, speaking in both Spanish and English, as he announced his intention to win a seat in the legislature representing the District of St. Croix.

His friend, Paul E. Joseph, editor of the *West End News*, saw him as a "frank speaking man," with a desire to secure the most for St. Croix. "He sees vast possibilities for improvement in this island....he would be happy to work with all members from St. Thomas and St. Croix to the end that improvement here may be realized." Frits promised his listeners "to concentrate on getting vocational training, and proper assistance for agriculture especially for the small farmers." He also wanted better airport facilities, saying those were only a few of the things he has in mind to work for should he be elected.

Ballots allowed voters to select two district candidates and two out of six at large candidates. As votes were counted on election day, 2 November 1954 Frits, the novice, ran first in St. Croix, out polling a veteran campaigner by forty–nine votes.

St. Croix District Candidates

Candidate	Votes	
Frits E. Lawaetz	616	newcomer
Eric Carroll	567	served five previous terms in Council
J. Wilfred Benjamin	559	served in the most recent Council
Aureo Diaz	552	newcomer
Alva McFarlane	546	served twice, 1949–1952
Regalado Benitez	440	newcomer
Axel Schade	352	served 1953–1954
C. Lloyd Joseph	155	newcomer

John Merwin and Walter I.M. Hodge of St. Croix won the minimum number of at large seats for St. Croix; while four at large seats were swept up by St. Thomas candidates: Joseph A. Gomez, Earle B. Ottley, Percival Reese, and Weymouth Rhymer, all Unity party men. District winners from St. Thomas were Lucinda Millin and Jorge Rodriguez. Julius E. Sprauve won in St. John. Unity party politicians were jubilant with their landslide in the St. Thomas district; they had accomplished what they predicted: domination of the new legislature and payback time for the governor.

The newly elected senators had little time for reflection as Governor Alexander called for the first working meeting to take place in St. Thomas at 8:00 P.M. on 29 November. It would take another six weeks for Frits to get his official notification of election from William F. Moorehead, chairman of the election board for St. Croix. It was dated 7 January 1955 and is one of his proud possessions. Frits's mother sat down on 3 November to write him a note congratulating him on his victory: "Do not forget to pray for help from above that God will give you wisdom and success in your duties so it will be a blessing both for yourself and for those you serve." Far, who had died nine years earlier, was not witness to his resounding victory.

— Chapter Twenty–Six —

Frits's Agenda for St. Croix

Governor Alexander's agenda for that November meeting was singular: this was an opportunity for the new senators to have their input in his budget.

Frits does not know whether Unity members or the Democrats responded, but he jumped in and conducted a serious examination in St. Croix for the most pressing needs of the people. Some ten years earlier an act of Congress (Public Law 510, Seventy–eighth Congress) had provided a $10 million public works program for the territory. After years of planning and hearings, many projects were being built: new hospitals, schools, creation of the seawall in Charlotte Amalie, potable water plants, sewer and salt water lines, modern telephone systems; miles of roadways were to be improved or built. The original amount had seemed staggering, but had been rapidly eaten up; many areas were still in need.

Frits wrote a three–page letter dated 3 January 1955 to Governor Alexander stating they had much, much more to do on St. Croix "for its future progress." Regarding health and sanitation, Frits said Frederiksted's new hospital was inadequate and the old building should be annexed to it after renovations — set aside $100,000. He wanted $30,000 for modernizing the King's Hill Poor Farm. North of Frederiksted, Pond Bush, a garbage disposal area which flooded regularly, needed better control, and he suggested creating trenches. Adjacent to Pond Bush area was a public beach and bathhouse; Frits wanted this area fenced and landscaped with toilets added. He also wanted toilets placed in the ball field where the one–legged, war veteran school principal, Mr. Benedict, had taught the children of Frederiksted the American game of baseball for so many years. Frits urged Governor Alexander to complete sewer systems for St. Croix's two towns, and hoped funds would be made available to provide loans for financing toilet installations and connections, so "we in the near future can forever forget the night soil truck." Frits included requests for comfort stations at the Christiansted ball park and by the fish markets in both towns, "especially for the benefit of the women who come to purchase fish and often have to wait considerable time for the arrival of the fishing boats."

For farmers he asked that the government correct an error made when a windmill was built in Grove Place gut where the wind seldom blew, noting that electric current was available and should be hooked into it to move water to the government's ten thousand gallon concrete dam and on to farmlands. Additionally, Frits wrote, "There are several areas where there is a concentration of small growers that water facilities can and should be made available. Some of these areas already have good wells, but no storage and piping facilities. $10,000," he said, "will go a long way in rectifying this situation."

Over the following decades, indeed up to the present time, his pleas for water storage and piping facilities were constant but seldom answered. There were a few senators who protested loudly at any effort they thought might benefit Frits Lawaetz, even though by the sheer size of Canaday's operation, Frits would never qualify as "a small farm operator." Without storage and piping, running a home farm meant hauling drums of water almost daily. Young people looked at this backbreaking labor and its low monetary return and turned away. Few men or women farm the flatlands today, because access to water is still an issue.

In another section of his letter to Alexander, Frits showed the expertise he had gained from years working on big operations, first with the United Puerto Rico Sugar Company, then, on St. Croix, at the River–Fountain complex and, lastly, Annaly Farms. All of those companies had access to the best American intelligence available in livestock and vegetative areas. Frits also was able to attend trade shows in Puerto Rico and elsewhere to hear and meet experts. In many cases, Frits was the expert and shared his knowledge freely as well. "Those trips and visits are not available to the small grower," Frits told the governor, "and there is the lack of both a top class horticulturist and a veterinarian on St. Croix." Frits shared all the knowledge he gained with his fellow cattlemen in St. Croix and the cane growers as well, but he said that nothing replaces on–site examinations and getting information in person. Frits demanded a first class veterinarian for St. Croix, not a second class vet as was planned. He argued for a fumigation plant so St. Croix products could be exported; he asked for marketing facilities for the small growers. "If equipment and good supervision is made available to the small grower, he will not alone produce more cane, so much needed now that the entire Virgin Islands economy depends on the revenue of rum; but will also be able to produce more fruits and vegetables so badly needed in our Islands. Our government institutions could be supplied at certain months of the year with locally raised products such as meats and vegetables, fruits, milk and eggs. The small grower is a very important citizen in our community, but in the latter years has suffered a lot due to lack of equipment and cooperation. He needs someone to help plan his farm...and also help with the marketing be it cane, vegetable or livestock." He pointed out that many countries set up depots where farm products are received and sold to the public at fair prices. Frits also strongly recommended closing the in–town slaughterhouses and replacing them with a federally approved abattoir, so people could be supplied with good, as well as cheap meat. Not least, a top athletic coach was recommended for the education budget and, he emphasized that "good vocational training is a must. What happened to the Veterans' vocations training?"

Highways and roadways also caught his attention. He told Alexander that, of the funds set aside for road work, priority should be given to the repair of the newly hard surfaced roads, because they were not lasting; in fact he felt the need for a full investigation, so a similar error would not recur. And he spoke, for the first time, about the desirability of a scenic road similar to the one along the ridges of St. Thomas, "so our Island people may have an opportunity to see their beautiful Island and take pride therein, and visiting tourists the opportunity to see the beauty of the Island, that was once called 'The Garden of the West Indies.' " Frits suggested the road run from Salt River ridge over Clairmont and Mt. Eagle across Bodkin and Spring Garden to end at Ham's Bay. He thought $50,000 would be needed for an engineering survey and trail.

Not least, he asked that the public beach area at Altoona Lagoon, set aside in 1951, be developed with facilities for the residents of Christiansted. He complemented the governor, because final arrangements were completed for the extension of the runway at St. Croix's international airport. As if he had not presented a banquet table full of projects, Frits closed with these remarks: "As I get more acquainted with the needs of the Islands and its people I will always be glad to present them for your kind consideration. May the New Year bring close cooperation and understanding to us who have been given the privilege to serve and govern the people of these islands that they may prosper in the years to come." Frits may have been a freshman senator, but he was focused.

Members of the First Legislature repeated their oath of office after District Court Judge Herman E. Moore on the afternoon of 10 January 1955. The legislature was then located on the third floor of St. Thomas's library building on Main Street, site of the previous municipal council chambers. It was the beginning of a whole new career for Frits.

Frits at senate work

— Chapter Twenty–Seven —

Reflections on the Legislature

"Working in the legislature as a senator was a wonderful life in many ways. Because you were in a position where with a little phone call you could help people who thought they had a mountain in front of them." When Frits entered office in 1955, it was supposed to be a part–time job paying $600 a year; Alexander's proposed budget was $4 million; the territorial population was about 28,000, and Frits knew just about every adult in St. Croix. By the time of his retirement in January 1979, the job was full time, paying $15,000 and senators were making decisions involving a general fund budget of $117.7 million for a population which had grown to 96,569 people, triple that of 1960. (In January 1979, senate salaries were increased to $25,000, the same as the lowest paid commissioner.)

Frits says it was an amazing thing, "watching the island of St. Croix grow and grow out of the sugar cane industry into an industrial and tourist–based business." But that tremendous growth and conversion did not evolve out of thin air; it was the result of strong economic growth in the United States, coupled with foresight and long–term planning on the part of the senators, as well as appointees in the Department of Interior and the president's man in Government House.

For St. Thomas, the fast–paced postwar boom began to pay off. Following recommendations of the economists reports from the 1920s, the federal government had directed its efforts to promoting St. Thomas as the "Shopping Mecca Of The World," luring cruise ships in large numbers every month. The overthrow of dictator Fulgencio Batista in Cuba in 1959, nationalization and the subsequent closing of Cuba to American tourists in 1962 helped make St. Thomas the premier Caribbean cruise ship destination for the next forty years.

Unity party members dominated the First Legislature: Earle Ottley, Percival Reese, Joseph Gomez, and Weymouth Rhymer were from St. Thomas, Julius Sprauve from St. John. They were joined by Walter Hodge and Eric Carroll from St. Croix. Democrats Lucinda Millin and Jorge Rodriguez of St. Thomas, along with John Merwin, a Republican, and Frits, an independent, became the minority representatives. As the first order of the day following their swearing in, Hodge was elected president; Ottley, vice–president; and Rodriguez, secretary.

The most pressing thing they had to accomplish was merging the two district's laws into one Virgin Islands code. Many would see that as a simple task, but it was not. For examples: St. Croix had the death penalty for murder, St. Thomas–St. John did not; St. Croix had no deep water pier, while a great deal of federal funds went towards keeping the privately–owned Havensight docks in St. Thomas busy. Another complication was a longstanding battle between the old municipal councilmen and appointed governors for authority to name members of boards and commissions and to approve gubernatorial appointments. The second, and normally routine, act they needed to undertake was passage of the budget for the fiscal year beginning 1 July 1956.

The first session proved that the majority had no intention of letting the appointed governor, Archie Alexander, reduce their authority as implied in the 1954 amended organic act. When the government budget was sent down to the legislature on Main Street for approval, the majority created a separate appropriation for each department and went so far as to withhold appropriations for education, public works and insular affairs. In addition to the revised budget, the legislature as a whole passed a number of bills to increase wages, provide annual leave to government employees, revise the pension system, build middle–income housing, and establish day care centers. As Ottley said in his biography, *Trials and Triumphs*, "When we rejected several of the governor's legislative proposals and adopted our own versions, there was a flood of veto messages. Alexander disapproved so many bills — more than forty in the 1955 regular session alone."

Frits was not included when these changes were made by Unity party senators and allies. He was elected and behaved as an independent and, with his own agenda, had geared up for action. It soon became apparent that Frits was spinning his wheels. Frits's bills were being drafted by the legislative counsel, Antoine Joseph, and they were being sent to the appropriate committee. However, despite Frits's constant urging, the chairman of the Rules Committee did not put them on the agenda. By the end of the sixty–day session Frits was discouraged. Just attending was a hardship. Crucian members of the legislature had to fly over to St. Thomas at the beginning of each week, in time for the start of the evening session. Meetings during the session often went until long after the last flight had left for St. Croix. A man accustomed to standard Crucian fare and his own bed, Frits was boarding in a room and taking meals out in restaurants on a expense account of ten dollars a day. Furthermore, Frits was not a young man like Ottley, who was thirty–four years old and a pro with eight years of experience. Frits was forty–eight, with a bad leg, a bad kidney and all the aches and pains of a career cowboy. Despite the hardship, Frits was filled with the conviction that it was his duty to serve. He also was used to being in charge and making decisions and had little experience with being thwarted by men whom he thought should be aiming in the same direction — for the betterment of their community. He knew first hand what it took to operate a farm, what was needed in the hospitals, what had to be done to improve the condition of St. Croix roads, the need to channel young boys' and girls' energies into productive directions and train them well for the future.

He also had humility. Frits finally went to Earle Ottley whom he had correctly perceived to be the power house of the Unity team and asked him what he was doing wrong that no bill of his had yet made it onto the agenda of the Rules or Finance committee. Earle had become fond of Frits and respected both his clarity of thought and his fairness, so he took the time to tell Frits, "You are young and you don't understand this system. You hold no debts for us." He advised Frits to tell the senators who had bills in his committee when they were coming up and to let them know he was voting for them. When the time came for that senator to consider a bill from Frits, he would get the vote returned. "It was not quite as simple as that," said Frits, "but Earle took the bills I wanted included in the budget, and the next day they were passed without the committee process. I learned my lesson. At home I was used to ordering folks around but here, I was just one among equals."

Frits learned to compromise, and, as needed, he voted with the Democrats or with Unity party members. But Frits did not relinquish his integrity. He had run as an independent, so he had no ties to old politicians and old influences, and he would continue to run independently for a total of five elections. He did not like the confrontational, insulting actions of many who had served before in municipal councils. He didn't like the tricks that had been played and wanted to stand clear of the race–baiting tactics used against Washington appointees, and he was able, all through his public career, to do so. Part of his philosophy was that, "People should be able to depend on you; bills should be based on the real needs of this island. I don't like to make promises I can't keep." Frits's firm and honorable convictions, which had been developed throughout his life's work, served him and the public equally as well in his many years in the legislature.

Governor Alexander began the practice of doing annual budgets for capital improvements, a change from the piecemeal approach of previous administrations. Most capital projects first came to the senate Public Works Committee for scrutiny. As a member of the Public Works Committee for many years, Frits was as focused as a breeding bull, not only identifying the funds to begin and complete his projects, but making sure funds were released as well as appropriated. When there were balances left over from a project, he could always find a need to be filled. He worries a lot about the committee system today, because some governors' financial people are not keeping the senators informed in detail about the status of appropriations and expenditures. "When you are in charge you should know every crab hole on this island. We knew where all the money was and what was not needed in a specific year. I don't know how the current legislature can operate without knowing what each fund holds in terms of money."

Although senate work was considered part time, Frits got to know every single employee in the departments he oversaw with the same dedication he had applied as a child to studying kitchen gardens. He learned not only the ups and downs and ins and outs of the work and the work places, but personal problems as well. And he worked as hard to resolve those problems for the lowest wage earner as he did for commissioners. "I was never in the legislature for my own personal gain. Prayers and thanks were enough."

— CHAPTER TWENTY–EIGHT —

The Early Years in the Senate

As part of his new career, Frits had done a complete assessment of the island, and his vision was simple, clear and long term: improve its infrastructure and train residents so they can prosper. He had learned the value of friends in high places during his years on the V.I. Soil and Water Conservation Board. He kept in touch with key congressmen who affected territorial areas: Senator Leo W. O'Brien of New York, chairman of the Subcommittee on Territory and Insular Affairs, and his counterpart Congressman Wayne Aspinall in the House, among others. When the secretary of the interior, the secretary of agriculture and the vice president visited the territory in March 1955, he was comfortable in meeting with them on an equal footing and from a position of knowledge that overrode his status as a new senator.

Among his first bills passed were provisions for: the addition of a wing to the new Christiansted hospital (later named after Governor Charles Harwood); commencement of work on St. Croix's Scenic Drive; an annex for the Frederiksted hospital; recreation facilities in Grove Place, Christiansted and Frederiksted; water development for small farmers; improved potable water distribution; sidewalks to the hospital and schools in Christiansted; completion of King's Hill Home; providing care of those suffering from Hansen's disease (leprosy); soil conservation measures, and a hospital wing for the chronically ill.

Every year he was in the legislature, Frits supported the community bands with $1,500 for instruments and uniforms for the three main towns of Charlotte Amalie, Frederiksted and Christiansted. By 1956, he also had supported adoption of the fair labor standards; the right to send a non–voting delegate to the Congress of the United States; a workmen's compensation act; authorization for construction of a deep water pier in Frederiksted; and the Ottley–Richards Land and Home Loan Act of 1956.

A very important bill for Frits was one requesting that the Department of Interior approve the establishment of a St. Croix Port Authority. As a measure of his esteem, Frits was personally notified by phone and letter, on 30 May 1956 by Anthony T. Lausi, director of the Department of Territories, that the undersecretary of interior, Clarence A. Davis, had that day granted approval to establish the St. Croix Port Authority. The St. Croix airport and new pier were important to Frits as tools to provide new opportunities for employment for his people. He thanked the governor for his attention and also let him know that Ward Canaday had sent cables to the President of the United States, to Secretary Weeks of Commerce, and to the Civil Aeronautics Administration about continuing funding for the territory's airports.

Frits urged his peers to join his battle to get full funding for the St. Croix airport, as St. Thomas would not be ready for construction for another five to six years. The counterpart to support for that required him to vote in February 1956 for a half–million dollar waterfront highway project in Charlotte Amalie, for $106,000 to renovate the old marine barracks into a legislative hall, and for incidental repairs to Government House in St. Thomas. He also worked hard to pass a $707,808 appropriation to create a new elementary and high school in Frederiksted which would later be named for Claude Markoe.

A couple of other momentous acts took place in 1956: the first group health insurance plan was established for government employees; Laurence Rockefeller offered, and the National Park Service accepted, his gift of nearly seventy–five percent of the Island of St. John as a park; St. Thomas and Christiansted harbors were to be dredged; the deep water pier for Frederiksted was approved on 21 June with the bond ceiling set at $1.25 million as the first act of the new St. Croix Port Authority; and the old Benedict Air Field expansion was underway. Frits attended the new Harwood hospital and Christiansted high school openings and was there when the lepers' home in Richmond was closed forever and its few remaining patients transferred to the Carville Institute in Louisiana. So much was falling into place, he felt good.

The difference in objectives between Unity senators and Frits Lawaetz were clear cut: the Unity group, led by St. Thomian Earle Ottley, was locked in a clash with Governor Alexander over control of government employees and appointments, most of which were in the St. Thomas–St. John district. Lawaetz felt the role of the legislature was two–fold: (1) to provide tools to independent workers, so they could improve their lives and livelihoods and succeed in the private sector, and (2) to provide fair treatment for all workers, including government employees. Most of the time the two objectives did not interfere with each other, so Frits, for the most part, was not perceived as a threat by Unity members.

But there were other areas of concern. By the end of 1955, it was evident to Frits and many Crucians that the revised organic act put St. Croix at a tremendous disadvantage. The majority of the seats in the unicameral legislature were elected at large, but voters were limited to voting for just two of six candidates. The main islands had fixed seats as well: two each in St. Thomas and St. Croix, one in St. John. In the first election in November 1954, St. Thomians dominated with six residents elected — two for district seats, four at large. St. John elected one, and just four came from St. Croix, forty miles to the southeast. Equally as important to the election process, control and power over strictly local issues had been taken from the local arena and firmly planted in the capital. John Merwin, a Republican, and Frits, an independent, were newcomers to the legislative process; the other two from St. Croix, Walter Hodge and Eric Carroll, were old hands at it, but they too were not vital or involved in the committee process, only for actual votes because, by private agreement following adoption of the rules of the legislature, Hodge was given care of the St. Croix office, and Ottley as vice president ran St. Thomas, where all the action took place. Another issue was power over the appointment of commissioners and members of boards and commissions; senators had no say. Furthermore, the governor's appointments to key positions were mostly residents of St. Thomas, a move that left many, Frits included, deeply annoyed. Observers remarked that in all ways St. Croix was being treated like the unwanted brother.

Taking the issue to the national level, Frits made his objections to revised organic act's mandates the prime point of his speech before the U.S. House of Representatives Committee on Interior and Insular Affairs meeting in December 1955. He said at the meeting, held in Christiansted, that "in the largest island of St. Croix there were no Commissioners, no assistant Commissioners...not even an Administrator with Cabinet Rank." He pointed out that, in Executive Order #2, Reorganizing and Consolidating the Executive Branch of the Virgin Islands, issued by Governor Alexander, there was the stipulation that each department would have a gubernatorially appointed assistant commissioner, but that was never put into effect. Frits also wanted St. Croix to have an administrator who sat on the governor's cabinet. He pointed out that even senators from St. Croix had to get information on the simple day–to–day operations of the government by going to or writing to the government offices in St. Thomas.

Readers today would perhaps find it hard to fathom the frustration then, given our current use of facsimile, e–mail and air travel. In the 1950s and 1960s the formal manner of communication was, if not in person, through a written message. The telephone was useful, going through the central exchange, but serious matters were always committed to paper. Paper meant postal transmission, by plane or by sea, a matter of days between the islands. For a few messages, telegrams or the telex machine was used, mainly by newspapers and air and sea schedulers. Island residents had been told that the 1954 federally–mandated unicameral legislature was logical, because the islands did not have enough residents to warrant separate local governing bodies. (That logic had failed in 1852 under Danish rule.) Residents in St. Croix did not believe that St. Thomas or St. John representatives knew enough or cared enough to make good decisions about the small simple needs of their area, like road repairs or water catchments. Past experience had proved that belief true. Future events were to support their belief again and again and raise constant friction during budget allocation sessions.

In addition to registering his concerns about inequities in the election process, Frits spoke before congressional committee on the need to improve the St. Croix airport and docking facilities for the tourist trade. At that time the federal aid for the airport stood at $300,000 annually for four years, matched locally by $100,000 in each of the four years. Frits told the committee that the Civil Aeronautics Administration had approved the master plan for St. Croix, which included demolition of the old Benedict terminal building and construction of a new one with a good access road, strengthening the runway and increasing it from five to six thousand feet, fencing and such for a total of $770,000. Frits asked the House committee to add another $30,000 for a hanger. He asked that the first two years of appropriations be assigned to St. Croix which had an approved plan and then assign to St. Thomas the last two of the four–year monies, as by then they should have an approved plan for their upgrading. He also recommended that the entire island be upgraded and prepared for tourism, that general roads be repaired and scenic roads built along the ridgeways, as well as the docking facilities developed.

Frits made sure the House members were informed of the tremendous improvements to water storage capacity on St. Croix, due to the dam building program undertaken over the past two years by the Virgin Islands Corporation (VICORP), a federal instrumentality working in conjunction with the local Soil and Water Conservation Board. Before that program began, St. Croix had a dam capacity of four hundred thousand gallons. He thanked Congress for the fact that the islands now had seventy dams with a capacity of several million gallons of water, raising the water table considerably and improving standing wells. He urged the program be continued. (Frits modestly failed to take credit for getting those dams in the first place as chairman of the Soil and Water Conservation District.) He reminded them of the urgent need for additional housing for low and moderate income earners, especially in Frederiksted. Ever the master communicator, Frits made sure the committee members were able to get around the island for a tour and a taste of island cuisine and music with a little reception at Annaly.

— Chapter Twenty–Nine —

Friction

In the course of his first term Frits often had a "baptism by fire" in the legislature, but he could see results flowing into the development of St. Croix that would finally make life easier for her people, some thirty–eight years after the transfer when many islanders thought that affiliation with the United States would bring instant prosperity to their desperate shores. The new governor, Walter A. "Roy" Gordon, committed himself to working with the legislature. The secretary of interior kept one official or the other close to his side to make sure Washington's instructions were followed. Alexander's directive to his department heads, which had forbidden them to provide any information or to appear before the legislature without his personal written consent, was quickly reversed, presumably upon an order from Interior. There were still some hangovers from the past. In addition to the question of whether government officials had to respond to legislative committees, Interior interpreted the revised organic act to mean that the legislature's sole power to meet existed during their annual sixty–day session. Interior refused to pay per diem expenses incurred during hearings and meetings for committee work. The legislature filed suit and in August 1956, the district court ruled that the legislature and its committees and their authority did exist outside of the specific days set aside for session and that subpoenaed officials had to appear with any requested official documents and records. Members of the legislature celebrated their vindication.

Gordon's term of office became confrontational when the Virgin Islands Code was presented and passed, including a portion which Gordon termed unacceptable: that certain nominations to boards and commissions be subject to legislative approval. Gordon vetoed it; the legislature overrode; when sent to President Eisenhower, he upheld Gordon's veto. The stage was set once again for battle.

Before battle with Gordon was undertaken, the battle for reelection began. On several occasions during 1955 and 1956, Frits had taken time on bandstands and on the radio stations to report to the people on the state of the territory, from his perspective. He promised to "unselfishly work towards a better understanding between the legislature and the governor, however never at the expense of the rights of my people." Frits clearly abhorred the problems being raised by the lack of cooperation and political difficulties between the governor and members of the legislature. He said elected Virgin Islanders must have the respect and confidence of their own people to gain that of fellow Americans in Congress, Interior and the Executive Branch. He stated that he was sure "every man in Congress is anxious to give us the rights due us as American citizens, to have a representative in Congress, elect our own governor and [determine] how moneys granted us should be spent. However," he said, "none of this will be given us until Congress is convinced that we are ready and willing to send representatives to the legislature who will live up to American principles and defend the rights of all its citizens, rather than to have men who crave for party and political powers and are anxious to make every citizen subordinate to its party and its henchmen." Frits said that can only lead to encouragement of dictatorship. And the gauntlet was thrown down before the Unity senators. He went on to note that ninety–five percent of his bills were unanimously passed and adopted by the legislature. Frits also freely admitted that he had voted "no" to many bills presented by other senators, called them undemocratic and contrary to good government and contrary to the organic act.

One of the battles that was important to Frits in that election was the usurping of all of the airport funds by Interior and redirecting them to the St. Thomas runway. The U.S. Senate had passed the allocations as Frits had requested: the first two years were to go to the St. Croix approved plan, the last two to St. Thomas. Interior cut part of the St. Croix appropriation. Frits said the cut by Interior "will *not* take care of our needs and that if the St. Croix runway was not lengthened and strengthened immediately, the Virgin Islands will lose a large bulk of the tourist trade, as these planes will bypass us and establish routes to other Islands." He referred to his political independence, saying that, although membership had been offered by all four major parties, "I believe in the policies of political parties, but having very little experience in politics I am not convinced myself as yet what party I can best serve you in. Until such time, I believe I can best represent you as an independent candidate. During the last two years I was always willing to cooperate with any senator regardless of party, provided I believed the senator's intentions were sincere and for the better of our people." Frits ended every request for support with thanks for giving him the privilege and honor of representing the people during the last two years, and said, "I hope you were satisfied with my work and will again give me your support on November 6." He never forgot that his efforts were constantly being rated and that he "served, not deserved."

— Chapter Thirty —

The New Majority

Frits won reelection to his district seat; Walter I.M. Hodge was reelected at large, and two new comers from St. Croix won. Dr. Aubrey Anduze, a Department of Health dentist, a rookie, won the Christiansted district seat, and Ron DeLugo, a Democratic party organizer from St. Thomas, now a resident of St. Croix, took the second at large position. Ousted were: Unity party member Eric Carroll of Christiansted, who had served in the Sixteenth and Seventeenth Municipal Council as well as the First Legislature, and Jorge Rodriguez of St. Thomas, an unaligned first termer. In St. Thomas–St. John, Theovald E. Moorehead, a Democrat, was elected because of the retirement of Julius Sprauve. The Unity party had lost two guaranteed supporters, and the legislature two experienced men.

The winners met before the opening session to align themselves for control. An informal coalition of Democrats (DeLugo and Anduze from St. Croix, Moorehead from St. John and Lucinda Millin of St. Thomas) were joined by minority representatives (Lawaetz and Merwin) to become the majority in the Second Legislature. Rookie Aubrey Anduze was elected president and Lucinda Millin, vice president. Frits worked with the majority team on most legislation, he recalls, and says that, with issues so important to all of them, the entire legislative body was mostly going in the same direction. Tourism was booming with 130,000 visitors a year and $15 million gross expenditures, triple that of just four years before. Even more telling was comparison to the pre–World War II years when they had boasted about fourteen thousand tourists a year in St. Thomas and thirty regular cruise ship calls there. With a burgeoning population, new schools were being built, but even more space was needed. Progress was measured also by the first direct dial telephone call being made between St. Thomas and St. John on 9 April 1957.

The Democratic majority, with which Frits was an active player, set impressive bench marks for others to follow, and Frits was able to move some of his key programs through the legislature. For the small farmers, he got a new dam project by Bethlehem's central factory area in St. Croix; water storage and piping facilities funding was increased. In May 1957, a new seventy–unit low–income housing project was authorized for Frederiksted (now Harrigan Court), to provide homes for anticipated workers on the new pier. The federal government agreed to create the Bassin Triangle housing in 1957 and also housing at Richmond (sometimes called "Red Brick," later named for David Hamilton Jackson), for a total of 170 low–rental units just west of Christiansted. A major health concern was removed with relocation of the night soil dump out of Frederiksted and an end to pit privies in the town. Act 302 authorized day care centers, first funded by profits from the Virgin Islands lottery. The St. Croix Workers Labor Union donated pasture land at Grove Place for creation of the playground and park built there.

Stabilizing the economy was important, and with majority party support, the Emergency Molasses Fund Act passed in June 1957. This act provided that rum factories had a cost ceiling of seven cents per gallon on molasses. Any costs over that amount would be paid from the fund. Now Virgin Islands rum manufacturers were able to compete with other countries and islands which did not have minimum wages, health and safety standards or were subsidized by their governments. It proved a wise move. The subsidy funding came as a provision of the Revised Organic Act of 1954, in section 28(b) which allowed the local government to get an excise tax return of $10.50 for every proof gallon of rum shipped. This return brought in $3.5 million in 1957. By 1960 it would nearly double to $6.5 million. These excise tax returns became a major factor in the territorial budget, providing a staggering largesse to build schools, libraries, roads and hospitals.

Unfortunately, work on the St. Croix airport stalled with public opposition to several points, one of which was the federally required three–mile surround occupancy exclusion requirement. Another sticking point came up when the Chamber of Commerce did not like its exterior design. Yet another problem was lack of interest on Acting Governor Merwin's part. Frits wrote the director of the Office of Territories in Washington late in November 1957, that he was afraid the V.I. would lose those funds if there was further delay, since the CAA had provided seventy–five percent of the funding. He told Lausi, "I spoke very firm with the Governor on this issue, but he did not seem to agree on its urgency....I am therefore asking your help in getting this most vital project going." Lausi agreed that delays were a problem, but the CAA and Interior were trying to address the concerns of the local people as much as possible. Lausi assured Frits that funding would remain available until expended.

By early December, there were two proposals ready to bring back to St. Croix for a second round of public hearings. David Kelly, CAA regional director in Miami, arrived on St. Croix 12 December 1957 to personally handle the presentation. As Lausi said, "[Interior] can no longer tolerate any further delay." The St. Croix airport was declared completed in August 1960, and the Legislature of the Virgin Islands was able to move funds over to St. Thomas for Truman Airport's extension, which had been in the planning stages for several years. Mixed signals, a proposed change in the airport's location, problems with development of the fledgling College of the Virgin Islands (now the University of Virgin Islands) immediately north of the runway, and a host of other issues would drag out completion of the St. Thomas project until the mid–1990s.

During this Second Legislature, an old battle with the Office of Territories was finally settled over vouchers covering twenty–two days of per diem payments for the senators' work between sessions. Interior had rejected them in June 1956, saying the legislature would have to prove that incurred costs covered attendance at actual sessions. Lausi further threatened to disallow expenses incurred during special sessions, and the war of words between President Hodge and Lausi raged for nine months. Paying out of pocket for the unreimbursed expenses of travel, hotels and meals was a financial hardship for those members who had to travel from St. Croix by propeller airplane (forty miles each way) or from St. John by ferry and at times to stay overnight. But the battle was a critical one of who controlled the legislature — Interior or the local people — and it was eventually won by the legislature through the courts.

Funding for engineering services and construction on Frits's Scenic Drive project, first recommended in January 1955, was introduced in on 24 April 1957. Another housing project south of Frederiksted was approved in May 1957, which would be named for Walter I.M. Hodge in honor of his long years of public service.

The legislature began also to look at renewing the charter of the Virgin Islands Company. VICO, as it was called originally, had been established in 1934 to modernize the territory, build public projects such as roads, sewers, hospitals, power plants and the like. Through its projects on St. Croix, VICO paid two dollars a day for agricultural labor, the highest rate in the history of the Virgin Islands. In June 1949 it was federally reorganized into the Virgin Islands Corporation (VICORP). Included in its new charter was a seat specifically set aside for a sugar grower in the territory. Ward Canaday held that seat. VICORP essentially took over the property and activity of its predecessor, VICO. In a letter to the legislature, Norman Skeoch, president of the St. Croix Chamber of Commerce, noted that the 1949 charter would expire on 30 June 1959. He asked the legislature to push for at least another ten years of charter, pointing out that VICORP "is vital to the basic economy; employs many people year round; is the only outlet for 350 small farmers who supply roughly forty–five percent of the cane that is ground at Bethlehem; the molasses is the chief supply of the islands' distillers; internal revenue taxes are the main source of revenue for the islands; it operates the electric power plant, and our merchants benefit for direct sales." Governor Gordon and later Governor Merwin strongly supported extending the charter. The legislature also sent resolutions to the U.S. Congress in support of its continuation.

Also passed in 1957 was another critical piece of legislation: the Unified Tax Exemption Law, written to attract investment capital for economic development and to promote tourism and housing projects. The Unified Tax Exemption Law was the result of merging and amending two old industrial incentive acts from the predecessor district municipal councils. St. Croix had established a tax exemption scheme in 1952, St. Thomas in 1954. A commission was formed to serve the purposes of the act which would complement work being undertaken by federal action in the areas of low–income housing, water conservation and sanitation, and the St. Thomas airport.

— Chapter Thirty-One —

Passage of the V.I. Code

Perhaps the most important and controversial bill of the Second Legislature was approving the Virgin Islands Code. An initial version passed the legislature in 1956, but this was vetoed by Governor Gordon. The legislature appealed to President Eisenhower; but Gordon's veto was upheld by the president. Governor Gordon resubmitted the code to the Second Legislature on 6 May 1957 deleting the section requiring confirmation by the legislature of governors' appointments to boards and commissions. Governor Gordon had also stripped the legislature's restrictive terminology in budget bills, setting the stage for a confrontation. On Thursday, 9 May, the legislature adopted a motion made by Senator Ottley and seconded by Senator Reese to institute proceedings in the U.S. district court to determine (1) the legality of the governor's method of vetoing appropriations bills, and (2) the status of persons now serving on boards and commissions, appointed without confirmation by the legislature.

Members were in harmony on those two issues but the Judiciary Committee report, which had triggered this challenge, also carried the recommendation that bill 425, To Enact the Virgin Island Code, be passed. The Unity faction insisted bill 425 include confirmation of appointments, and prohibit the governor from using selective word veto powers; majority members wanted to leave those issues alone until the district court could make its determination. Compromise was reached with the approval of filing a law suit, but the arguments were not over or even strictly local. Democrats in Congress, including Leo W. O'Brien, chairman of the House Subcommittee on Territorial and Insular Affairs, were urging the V.I. legislature to pass the V.I. Code and send separate legislation to Congress for revising the organic act.

In a 9 May session, at 5:00 P.M., Senator Merwin moved the legislature adopt bill 425, enactment of the V.I. code. The Unity party members began their filibuster as promised. Battles raged for days over reading the entire 2,481 pages into the record. Senator Walter Hodge led for the opposition, declaring that Virgin Islands legislators, like legislators in U.S. states, should have the same rights to confirm appointments and subpoena witnesses. Hodge said, "...a lot of people — who are behind us, who are behind the members of this legislature to pass the Code, without the provision for legislative confirmation — have no roots here. They have no birthrights! in these Virgin Islands." Hodge said boards could be loaded with all types of people from any kind of community in the United States of America.

Hodge also charged that he had heard that senators would be forced to attend the session (to vote on the bill). He then asked to be excused from hearing the bill by incorporation, but this was denied. Upon reconvening on Monday afternoon, 13 May, Hodge immediately gained the floor when correspondence concluded to fend off passage of the V.I. Code by incorporation. President Anduze challenged Hodge's assertion that "to not read all pages into the record would destroy the rights of the people," noting that Hodge and the First Legislature "had done that same thing two years ago, without reading it into the record." Hodge countered by saying he would exercise his right to do so now. Ottley spoke next, telling the audience that the Judiciary Committee report carried only the signature of its chairman; committee members had no chance to sit down and discuss it; Ottley called it a "railroading" and declared he had hundreds of amendments to make, and like DeLugo, he was prepared to sit there until Christmas to be heard.

Senators Gomez and Rhymer also spoke against adoption by

incorporation, both declaring they would not remain in chambers unless the entire code was read. Senator Gomez challenged President Anduze to use the Sergeant at Arms to bring him back. Senator Rhymer reminded the body that under Conrad Corneiro's chairmanship, the municipal council of St. Thomas and St. John spent three months reading their existing code into the record.

Judiciary Committee chairman, Senator John Merwin, reminded the body that, with the exception of three new senators, the remaining eight had voted on the code twice before without a reading, that indeed he had been forced to consider budget bills with just one or two days notice, and was obligated to act on faith in those who forwarded them for action. Senator Ron DeLugo noted for the record that the filibuster was predicted by members of the Unity party time and time again after losing November's elections, saying that they (Unity members) could stop the majority in two ways, by walking out and breaking the quorum to act, or by forcing a vote requiring two–thirds majority to pass. Many heated words were flung about.

When St. Thomas members attempted to change the traditional 2:00 P.M. start of the session to post–dinner night work, Senator Lawaetz said he saw no reason for a night session and argued for starting sessions in the mornings. He eloquently stated that St. Croix people had had to take an early plane to St. Thomas that arrived by 8:00 A.M. but they were then kept waiting for sessions to start until 2:00 P.M. in accord with an old tradition. He would work twelve hours or more a day but would not waste the time each day from eight in the morning until two in the afternoon. (There were few interisland flights at this time.) Senator Hodge said he would not attend morning meetings, regardless. The body attempted to reconvene at 10:00 A.M. on Tuesday, 14 May but did not have a quorum, so the session began, as usual, at 2:00 P.M.

Upon advise of counsel, at the end of the Tuesday afternoon meeting, the president recessed until the following morning at 10:00 A.M. Anduze reopened the meeting at 10:55 A.M., on Wednesday, 15 May as a continuation of the Tuesday afternoon session; no member of the minority was present. He declared, "Since our regular legislative day is at 2:00 P.M. if there are no objections we shall leave today's roll call until that time and proceed with unfinished business. No objections came from majority members. After a short session as a committee of the whole, Merwin rose, stating that the committee of the whole, by unanimous consent, made certain amendments: first, to set an expiration date of 1 September 1957 for all incumbents on boards and commissions; second, to strike all reference to appointments by the governor and leave the question of appointments untouched by the code. These two points were major concessions to objections of the minority members who did not wish to give even the appearance of allowing what no other state allowed — appointments without advise and consent of the legislative body. Merwin then asked the president to consider all work on the code complete.

In a second strategic move, the body went into the committee of the whole once more and declared further reading of bill 425 be dispensed with and that any amendments to be offered be offered now. No amendments being made, the next step was to "special order the bill" at 2:00 P.M. immediately following roll call and "call the previous question" without any intervening vote or debate. The whole maneuver was completed at 11:45 A.M. by unanimous consent.

At 2:20 P.M., minority members of the legislature Gomez, Hodge, Ottley, Reese and Rhymer all answered roll call along with majority members Anduze, DeLugo, Lawaetz, Merwin, Millin and Moorhead. As soon as the president said, "Pursuant to the Special Order issued by unanimous consent this morning — at this morning's meeting — the House will now consider by roll call vote the passage of Bill 425." Ottley and Hodge were on their feet calling for a point of order. Anduze ordered the secretary, Mr. Holder, to continue roll call: Anduze voted yes; Mr. DeLugo voted yea; Anduze reported that Gomez was present but not voting, and there was a scramble to leave the room. (At that time no simple railing divided the room to define "the floor." One had to leave the room to be absent.) Mr. Hodge was stated as present and not voting, Lawaetz voted yea, as did Merwin, Millin and Moorehead. Only Ottley, Reese and Rhymer were able to exit fast enough to avoid being counted, but it did not matter – a quorum was present and the majority prevailed. Bill 425 passed on 15 May by six "yeas," two "present," and three "absent." Unity members began a verbal street war; DeLugo and Lawaetz in turn took to the streets of St. Croix to explain their position. Minority members boycotted the legislative session on 16 May when Governor Gordon hastily signed the V.I. Code into law.

There was one more attempt to cause mayhem over passage of the V.I. Code: on Thursday, 6 June following a dinner break at 7:45 P.M., "after working in an air of goodwill for two weeks to bury party differences and for progress" Senators Merwin, Moorehead, Anduze, Lawaetz and DeLugo returned from dinner at the nearby Lantern Restaurant to find Walter Hodge planted in the president's seat declaring himself "chairman pro tem" by popular consent. Ottley was appointed "secretary pro tem." Some spectators laughed but the minority members were dead serious. They rejected approval of the *Legislative Journal* and vowed to write the governor that the V.I. Code had been illegally passed. As Anduze demanded Hodge relinquish his seat, Hodge declared the session over *sine die,* and the five Unity senators piled into a car and fled into the night. It meant nothing legally; passage of the V.I. Code stood, but the point had been deftly hammered home that ignorance of parliamentary procedure and how to use it had cost a lot. The lesson was not forgotten. By January of the following year the provision to approve appointments "by advice and consent" to specific boards easily passed, resolving one of the minority issues.

— Chapter Thirty–Two —

Privatization of Services

By June 1957, senators were able to move into their new home, formerly the U.S. marine barracks, on the waterfront across from Fort Christian. Social welfare occupied the first floor, legislators took over the second with its broad "welcoming arms" staircase favored by photographers. Governor Walter A. Gordon gave his state of the territory address on 9 June 1957 as the inaugural speech in their new legislative hall. Gordon reported there was no unemployment and, due to Alien Work Bonds, the islands were able to keep up the fast pace of development. He said his major push would be improving the highway system on all three islands and completing the Scenic Drive on St. Croix. He reiterated that new water catchments and storage units were needed, as the Virgin Islands was going through another severe two–year drought, and he recommended the body consider distillation plants and new dams. In 1927, a much earlier effort to catch water was done by the U.S. Army Corps of Engineers. Creque Dam, built on St. Croix's north side, was expected to hold six million gallons of water for Frederiksted. Carl Lawaetz, among others, had given some of his land to provide a right–of–way for the aqueduct. Unfortunately the soil in that area proved unable to hold water, and a good storm was absorbed in less than six weeks. New systems were still critically needed. Desalinization, proven effective once again during World War II, was being pushed as the answer. Gordon said he had sent a ten–year plan to Washington for public works water and road projects, and, once approved by Interior, it would be submitted to the senators. It was a promising speech in an upbeat time. Frits and Donald Boreham, public works commissioner, traveled to Washington to testify as advocates for Gordon's programs before Senator Andersen's Public Works Committee in Congress.

All during 1957 and 1958, Senators Lawaetz, Anduze and DeLugo made a habit of speaking together at rallies and meetings about the state of the territory. They worked well together, both on and off the floor of the legislature, complementing each other's style, tireless in covering the island with their meetings. They built a tight team, kept the public informed, and built solid community support for their programs. In January 1958 the long disputed zoning law was adopted along with a building code, the result of dedicated effort by the Chambers of Commerce, the St. Croix Landmarks League and other associations, and the three Crucian legislators. On the down side to the boom, new construction had sent real property tax rates soaring. Newspapers recorded talk that speculators in St. Thomas were offering $45,000 per acre. Senator Lawaetz suggested a ten percent per year ceiling on increases unless improvements were made and that no hikes be made on agricultural land for a year following drought.

By May 1958 Ann Abramson replaced John Merwin as senator from St. Croix, as Merwin moved into the position of government secretary. With Morris DeCastro serving as acting governor, the top slots were held by men of the islands, a long desired goal of most islanders. Prosperity felt good to those who benefited and held out promises to those still waiting for it to come to their village. The pace of life was still peaceful, on Thursday (a half–day holiday for the private sector) and Sunday afternoons, community bands held concerts in the public parks for all to enjoy.

In June 1958 senators agreed to sell off the government–owned telephone company. The winning bidder was the International Telephone and Telegraph Corporation (ITT), founded in 1920 by St. Thomas native Sosthenes Behn, whose mother was a Monsanto.

ITT would be given exemptions on 9 October 1959, through act 504, on all taxes and fees for ten years to upgrade the system and extend services. Also approved that month in 1958 were two bus franchises: Ejnar Bolling was authorized to run Christiansted buses; all other routes were awarded to Rupert R. Abramson. Each bus franchise was for ten years. Senators Lawaetz, Abramson, Anduze and Millin also worked together to pass a bill buying fifty acres at Salt River with a $75,000 appropriation, and in July the governor signed into law act 350 naming Salt River an historic area.

Despite the upbeat times and apparent harmony, Frits went into his third senatorial campaign under a handicap, because he chose once again to run as an independent candidate. Unity party members wanted him out of the legislature, because he had consistently sided with the Democrat–run majority. On the other hand, Democratic party bosses wanted a man they could control. Thus, both factions campaigned against Frits. Complicating the Democratic campaign against Frits was the fact that Senator Ron DeLugo and Senator Aubrey Anduze, both St. Croix Democrats, worked very well with Frits but did not get along at all with the St. Croix Democratic district chairman, Henry Rohlsen. Rohlsen said Anduze was too powerful and that DeLugo had usurped his (Rohlsen's) power when he restructured Democratic clubs in St. Croix. Ron DeLugo had begun his political work in 1952 as a campaign manager and organizer for Lucinda Millin, his teacher in high school who inspired him and sparked his civic interest. He was just twenty–two years old when he helped reorganize Democrats in St. Thomas into a tight political body. In 1955 he moved to St. Croix and helped tighten up the party organization in both towns. According to Delta Dorsch, widow of the then Democratic leader in Frederiksted, this did not sit too well with Henry Rohlsen who did not want an independent Frederiksted club. As district chairman and head of the Christiansted club, Rohlsen wanted two vice presidents, one to serve each town. DeLugo ignored this and worked with Frederick Dorsch, one of the founders of the Frederiksted club.

At the start of the 1958 campaign, Henry Rohlsen publically demanded that Anduze and DeLugo stop supporting Frits and support their own ticket. By attending every one of their political events, Rohlsen made sure his candidates worked and campaigned only with the Democratic candidates. Frits was used to being the target of political attacks and handled those, but vicious private attacks from unknown sources began early into the campaign. His morals were questioned; his work for farmers was impugned as self–serving; he was said to be racist. One attack in particular threatened his life, and the police insisted he accept protection; he refused.

By himself, Frits went on the lecture circuit in both Spanish and English to tell people how he had gone to Washington on their behalf to get the Virgin Islands Corporation rechartered; he spoke about the bill in Congress to permit tax exemptions to anyone who invested $100,000 in hotels. He told them of improvements made in agriculture, in water facilities for the country and towns, and about new projects which were bringing in jobs. He spoke of better welfare assistance and school facilities for children, and said he hoped they would soon to have a chance to go to college right here on St. Croix. He spoke of his sponsorship of better harbor facilities and the deep water pier on St. Croix and improvements to the airport. Hamilton Airport bids were released in October 1958, and Frits was publicly thanked by Interior for his support in getting the specifications and plans approved locally. Frits won reelection, but power reverted to Unity party members; Anduze lost and Ann Abramson did not return. Candido R. Guadalupe won the second district seat from St. Croix. St. Croix was set back once again to a minimum of seats in the legislature.

— CHAPTER THIRTY–THREE —

The Federal Impact on Local Politics

Virgin Islands politics and government are both simple and complex. The simple part lies in developing a concept or program and gathering local support for it both throughout the districts and within the Legislature of the Virgin Islands. The complex part is the relationship between the local government and the federal government. Over the years most decisions and funds have come from the federal government. In the executive branch, responsibilities for the affairs of the U.S. territories fall under the Department of Interior. In the legislative branch, Congressional committees on the interior make decisions affecting the territories. Moreover, presidents of the United States appointed Virgin Islands governors.

Involvement of the White House, the Department of Interior and Congress in local affairs is frustrating enough. On top of that the time taken to accomplish any action can stagger the imagination. Delays which were normal in Washington were frustrating locally and, not incidentally, were used to help lose elections or create the impression that an old hand must be retained. The delays must have been seen as insulting when everything the Virgin Islands wanted had already been given to neighboring Puerto Rico at a much earlier date.

Puerto Rico became an American possession by an act of war

against Spain in 1898, not long before the United States bought the Virgin Islands from Denmark. Puerto Rico and the Virgin Islands sometimes worked together nationally for local rights, but the Puerto Ricans had a stronger lobby and more white American investments than did the Virgin Islands. President Truman had signed the Butler–Crawford bill in 1947 for Puerto Rico's public election of a governor and nearly every other official position. In 1958, the Virgin Islands governor was still chosen by the U.S. president. In 1950, Puerto Rico won the right to enact its own constitution. (Objections to these acts led to the assassination attempt on Truman's life that year.) Despite Puerto Rico's gains, things went much slower for the Virgin Islands, and its latest "constitution" (the Revised Organic Act of 1954) had been imposed by Congress.

Late in the 1950s however, with the Virgin Island's drive, still in progress, for an elected representative to the U.S. Congress and and elected governor, the need to toe national party lines became critical. Ralph Paiewonsky had served for years as Democratic national committeeman, Joe Alexander was Democratic state chairman and Mrs. Halvor Berg was the Democratic national committeewoman. Like their Republican counterparts, Stanley Farrelly and Erasmus Christian, these were people who used their own personal money to attend conventions. Despite national affiliation, it was not unusual for Paiewonsky or other leaders to publicly support their local favorites under whatever party name, because national parties did not have much impact on local matters. Now in the atmosphere of the late 1950s, it did matter. V.I. supporters in New York and Washington joined with politicians from the territory in again pushing for home rule: an elected governor, a delegate to Congress, more local control, and reapportionment of the V.I. legislature.

Gaining the right to elect a V.I. governor did not come easy. The V.I. legislators again petitioned for the popular election of a governor. Despite President Kennedy's support, beginning with his 1960 campaign, and despite placement of this issue in the

Democratic party platform, Congress did not act until 1968. Virgin Islanders elected their first governor, Melvin Evans, in November 1970, twenty years after Puerto Ricans first elected their governor.

A "Petition to Congress for a V.I. Representative in Congress" went out on 14 May 1958, and Senator James E. Murray of Montana surprised islanders by actually introducing a resident commissioner bill into Congress. A Home Rule Committee, similar to that which the councils had before 1955, was set up and funded by the legislature, to support the drive for electing a representative and a governor. The Home Rule Committee was comprised of seven V.I. senators and seven outside advisors, which allowed the legislature to continue to fund efforts of important politically connected associates residing in New York, like Caspar Holstein and Roger Baldwin of the NAACP.

The next year, President Eisenhower received much local praise for saying in his state of the nation address that he would recommend resident commissioner status for Guam and the V.I. as non–voting members to Congress. President Kennedy also supported election of a congressional delegate. Yet the issue stagnated year after year, in Congress after Congress.

For years, the V.I. legislature had sent Senator Ron DeLugo to Washington between sessions to lobby for a representative to Congress and on other matters. Finally, the legislature voted to set up an office in Washington until Congress funded the position. The first appropriation of $100,000 began 1 July 1968 for fiscal year 1969. Congress finally got moving when Senator Philip Burton introduced his bill for a V.I. delegate to Congress in March 1969, but passage was delayed until 8 May 1972. The people of the territory elected their first delegate in November 1972, after fourteen years of petition. Funds to pay for the costs of an unofficial delegate continued to be appropriated from local money until January 1973.

Another 1958 petition to Congress was for reapportionment of the legislature. Resolution 105 asked Congress to increase the number of voter choices to four seats at large, because voting for two of six positions, as was the case, "is unwise, unfair and not consistent with the development of a responsible party system." In March 1962, the V.I. legislature petitioned that the number of senators be set at three from St. Thomas, three from St. Croix, one from St. John and four at large, with all voters casting ballots for all four at large seats. A year later V.I. legislators asked Congress for an increase in their $600 a year salaries, because they were working on so many projects that their duties were like those of commissioners. Moreover, the high cost of living and inflation brought on by prosperity made their salaries inadequate.

In 1966 local legislators again urged Congress to support a bill to increase the number of senators in the V.I. legislature to fifteen. Congress did respond to this request, and in 1966 the people elected their first fifteen–member legislature.

Act 2253, approved 26 June 1968 established two districts and provided for electing six senators from St. Croix, seven from St. Thomas, provided one resided in St. John, and two at large who would be voted on by all the electors. This was a temporary allotment until the Virgin Islands had a census count for valid reapportionment. At the same time a Commission on Reapportionment was established in January 1968 with $50,000 to pay for the effort. Unable to complete the work in time, the temporary apportionment was extended to the 1970 election. Thereafter apportionment has been seven St. Thomas–St. John senators elected by residents of St. Thomas–St. John, seven Crucian senators elected by St. Croix voters, and one at large senator who must be a resident of St. John. Crucians objected, because it seemed their sister district had numerical advantage. Over the ensuing years there have been several calls for reapportionment based on the premise that the one–man one–vote rule was not being met.

It should be noted that, even today (2000), American citizens resident in the Virgin Islands still cannot vote for president of the United States. This is true also for U.S. citizens in other U.S. territories and in the District of Columbia.

— Chapter Thirty–Four —

More Trouble With His Leg

In August 1959, Frits was working on the farm just above his house at Annaly when he snagged his Jeep hard on a tree stump hidden by grass, severely damaging his knee. His leg did not heal; within days Frits knew that he was in crisis. The last time he had been examined in New York, Dr. Wilson had told him if there were any more problems Frits would lose his leg. Canaday insisted he come to Detroit and be examined at the Ford Hospital. Frits went up to Michigan alone and received bad news — his knee injury had reactivated the tumor on his tibia bone; the leg had to come off. Frits returned to St. Croix to talk to Bodil and make his decision.

In May his son Hans graduated with honors from Cornell University and then moved to work his last summer on a cattle farm in Florida. Hans, the senior member and colonel of his ROTC class at Cornell, had a promising military career ahead of him. When Frits returned from Michigan, Hans was home for just a few weeks before reporting to the U.S. Air Force pilot training school in Malden, Missouri. He recalls, "We drove up to the higher pastures and Dad asked me if I was interested in coming home to take over the farm. It was a major shock. At the time I was thinking of a career in the Air Force, had signed up for a five–year program. I knew I couldn't get out." But Hans made a commitment to his father that he would try, and whatever happened, he would go to Michigan after the operation and fly home with Frits. When his plane left St. Croix, Hans had even more time for thinking about his future:

avoiding a major storm, his plane was diverted to Venezuela and then around the southern Caribbean to San Antonio, Texas, while his car sat at the Miami airport. Hans made arrangements to retrieve his car, but he was not so lucky with his commander. He was told flatly that the Air Force did not train pilots for them to drop out, but he was allowed to change to a three–year program because of the crisis. While Hans's military career was being demolished, Bent was in his junior year at Stanford University in California, unable to help, and Fritsie was still in St. Patrick's elementary school.

Frits sadly went to Ford Hospital for surgery. Bodil was left home with Canaday's houseman, Ralph George, and foreman, Alfonzo "Wyson" Correa, to run her empty household and Annaly Farms, and to keep up with the monthly reports to Canaday. She knew Frits was depressed but could do nothing for that except keep in constant touch by mail and telephone. Word got around quickly about his condition. She sent him an article from the *Home Journal* in September 1959, which called him "a politician for whom even opponents have a kind word as an independent getting support from a broad cross–section of the St. Croix populace. Opponents have conceded that Lawaetz has a firm grip on the Crucian electorate. He is a good and constant mixer, who is equally at home in the exclusive tennis club or in the modest home of one of his rural constituents." It added, "Even before he became interested in politics, he sponsored baseball teams, seldom missed a game and accompanied teams to St. Thomas on inter–island series. Frits chaired the Public Works Committee in the 2nd and 3rd legislatures, and worked hard and conscientiously. Lawaetz never nurses a grudge and maintains good relationships with every senator, regardless of party affiliation. That is the reason why there was genuine regret expressed by so many people over his misfortune. There is widespread hope that he won't let this handicap get him down, but that he will face the future with characteristic optimism and high spirit." Sentiments like those and the many cards he received gave him comfort in his agony.

Frits was not only sad, but perhaps a little afraid as well. Frits had gone to Detroit in 1957 for removal of his ever–troublesome kidney, but his heart stopped on the operating table, so the surgery was postponed. He worried a heart attack might happen again. It did not, but his kidney problems remained, and two weeks after his leg amputation, Detroit doctors removed the problem kidney.

While in Detroit, Frits received hundreds of messages from islanders, an amount Ward Canaday thought staggering. Canute Brodhurst, owner and editor of the *St. Croix Avis* daily newspaper told some visiting reporters from Michigan to visit Frits on their return. They did and wrote up a full–page story on the senator. That story promoted a visit from the lieutenant governor of Michigan who made it possible for Frits, with a fancy police escort, to attend the state fair in a wheelchair. But recovery was hard work for a man his age. Frits said he would not come home until he could walk home, and he determined to do it by Christmas. Frits also recalls therapy as being the most painful experience in his life. He had to learn to use crutches again (he had spent two years on them in 1943–45), but this time he was off balance with an empty pant leg. He attended daily physical therapy designed to give him greater upper body strength and balance. His stump (cut above the left knee) had to be treated. He learned the agony of "ghost limb." After his prosthesis was built, he had aches and pain as he adjusted to the stiffness and tried to learn how to operate the knee and foot joints. And then he had to learn, once again, how to walk — this time on an unyielding "wooden" leg. His therapist Sally was a Tartar but caring, he says.

Hans got leave from the Air Force over Thanksgiving and went to Detroit to see his father. Hans saw firsthand how difficult recovery was for Frits. When Frits called a few weeks later and insisted he was ready to leave, Hans was prepared for the worst, for he remembered Frits couldn't walk alone. But Sally, the therapist, still had one final test for Frits before she would sign his release: that he walk in snow. December in Detroit is always bitter cold. On the day of his final test, "The grounds at the hospital were snowbound, the walkways were ice coated and it was into this environment Sally intended I would go or she wouldn't let me go home. I had a heavy winter coat over my pajamas and she made me go out into the yard, but she walked every step by my side. Then at the far end she turned me around and insisted I had to cross the open grassy area which was at that time under inches of snow. I told her I couldn't. She said I would never do anything if I couldn't do that, and she stepped away. I hated and feared every step, and when I fell, I thought I would never get up, but it was pride made me get up again, and when I finally made it back across the yard to do the door she came back by my side, and I think she had a little tear in her eye."

When Hans arrived at the hospital room some days later, still unsure how he would get his father home, the nurse told him Frits was down in the lounge as usual, entertaining all the rest of the patients with island stories. He had come a long way over the years from being known as the "Silent Dane" to a great and amusing storyteller, even with his heavy Crucian accent. Hans walked down that hallway. "Someone must have told my dad I was coming. He stood up and, unaided, started walking, slowly but surely, towards me. It was the best Christmas present."

All during his stay in Detroit, Frits had received cards and letters and hand–printed notes of sympathy. By the end of his nearly four–month stay, the number of letters had dropped to just a few each day. He was so grateful for the concerns, he had answered every one that had a return address. When Frits and Hans arrived in Puerto Rico, just before Christmas, he was delighted to see Bodil and young Fritsie there to meet him, he thought it was a great reunion. That night in Puerto Rico as Frits undressed, young Fritsie said "Me'son, that's a weapon you have there!" He said, "if anyone tries to attack you, well, just pull it off and let them have it" — a ten–year old boy's way of coping with such a great trauma. Frits was even more touched the next morning when he stepped off the plane in St. Croix at Alexander Hamilton Airport: a huge crowd had come to the airport to greet him. He has never forgotten that so many people were concerned for him.

— Chapter Thirty–Five —

The Party System

Frits spent the first months of 1960 learning how to do his everyday tasks with an artificial leg in his own environment. For a while he tried driving and shifting with a cane to hold down the clutch, using his right foot to press the gas pedal, but this proved rather dangerous in town, so he had to buy a car with automatic drive. During his therapy sessions in Detroit he had practiced stepping on uneven walkways, but all skills learned had to be conquered again in St. Croix with its centuries–worn brick paving and deeply curved gutters. Pastures were not easier, they sloped and provided different conditions when wet. He learned quickly, although he was exhausted by the end of each day and ached from the constant pressure on his stump. Frits could deal with that but found it nearly impossible to comfort young Fritsie who was traumatized by the explanation of the cause (cancer) and the loss of his dad's leg. Fritsie had avoided any questions about his dad while he was away and recovering from the operation. Later that year Fritsie had an appendicitis attack, and the family realized how deeply he was affected, for despite the pain in his side, young Fritsie insisted he had to have his leg removed too.

Making his own adjustments and trying to help his son relax, Frits caught up with his fellow senators on the progress of events while he was gone and began to prepare for the opening of the second half of the Third Legislature in April. Nineteen–sixty followed the pattern of the early years and saw several more dynamite changes. The churning evidence of prosperity was all about: down– islanders were coming in large numbers to fill vacant jobs; St. Thomas had a constant flow of tourists; families from America were moving in and restoring old greathouses in both districts; the Department of Interior was focused and in harmony with the senators, actively helping develop the territory through industrial incentives and new public projects. For workers, senators had the minimum wage level raised to sixty cents per hour, and shortened the work week to forty hours. They passed the first Executive budget to hit $10 million and started construction on Crown Bay's bulkhead in St. Thomas through issuance of industrial bonds worth $1.35 million. Another crowning achievement of that year was establishing the College of the Virgin Islands on 13 June 1960. Senators had instituted hotel and airport training in the vocational schools in January 1960; with a college approved, all doors of opportunity were opened to aspiring youngsters.

Party politics came into full bloom early in 1960. Republican President Dwight D. Eisenhower would leave office in January 1961, and an exciting race between Vice President Richard M. Nixon and Senator John F. Kennedy dominated the media both nationally and locally. Residents could congregate every week at local bars, in movie houses, or in Emancipation Park in St. Thomas and see film clips of the candidates' lectures. Residents also enthusiastically participated in local "lectures" which Frits loved to conduct. These were evening gatherings all over the islands held during sessions, where senators would talk about actions taken and how and why something occurred. During his own campaign at this time, again the outsider as an independent candidate but with clear links to the Democrats, Frits hit the circuit and spoke of improvements he and other senators were working on for the hard–working people of the territory. He told them of the achievements made in protecting farmers when the senators passed a bill requiring equitable allotment of homestead plots in June 1960. It provided that no added land allotments could be purchased unless one was not already a homeowner. The bill also restricted the home plot to a half–acre, with an overall five–acre farming limit. The buyer had to prove that he or she could farm and had to hold onto the land for twenty–five years; this was to end obvious cheating by speculators. For public health benefit, replacement of the in–town slaughterhouses with federally supervised abattoirs finally came to pass. For his hometown of Frederiksted, by 1960 funds were in place for eliminating the swamp known as Pond Bush. Long a source of mosquitoes and vermin who throve in the mucky garbage heap, this public works project was the start of reclamation of the north side of Frederiksted. Later in that same year, I. Gatewood James sold the government three acres to complete elimination of Pond Bush, and a playground was constructed near the Catholic church and elementary school, to serve it and the future Lagoon Street housing units.

The Lagoon Street housing project was part of an urban renewal plan set to eradicate decaying housing in the territory. There was great excitement when the V.I. legislature, authorized by the U.S. housing acts of 1949 and 1954, approved urban renewal projects on 10 December 1958, for St. Thomas, Christiansted and Frederiksted. Troubled for nearly one hundred years by neglect, due to lack of money, the towns were in terrible shape. Incomes had been too low for too long, and units lacked kitchen and toilet facilities. Ownership in many cases had been divided among many heirs, with or without benefit of wills, so much so that it was impossible in many cases for extended members of a family to agree to spend money on anything. In many cases households couldn't afford the upkeep. The U.S. housing act would eradicate the slums and allow for clean, new fully–equipped houses or apartments to be built in their place. In St. Thomas the urban renewal project got underway creating moderate–income units in Altona, Welegunst and Demerara. Its counterpart in Frederiksted, encompassing twelve blocks, would be delayed time and time again, although residents were bought out in the early 1960s. Most of Frederiksted's plan still lay aborning as late at 1999, but this first phase, completed in the late 1970s, created clean, modern three–story apartments for Frederiksted families. It is still a beautiful and bright light in the area.

In 1982, the Fourteenth Legislature honored Frits for his dedication and commitment to growth and development of the Virgin Islands by naming the Frederiksted apartment complex the "Frits Eduard Lawaetz Homes." Dedication was delayed for no apparent reason until the first Democratic governor, Alexander Farrelly, noted the lack and scheduled an official naming ceremony for the day after Frits's eighty–seventh birthday in 1994.

Still on the 1960 campaign trail, Frits reminded his constituents that by mid–1959 the move to remove all of the privy vaults, cesspools, and night soil cans in St. Croix was funded, and the process of hooking up private and public homes to underground public sewer systems in both towns was in high gear. Residents happily cheered and waved good–bye to the midnight "honey wagons." Frits reminded his listeners that the new special committee on the organic act, which was pushing Congress for more local self government, was made up of six senators under Earle Ottley's chairmanship. Three were from St. Croix, and one of these was Frits. He welcomed their recommendations on that important matter. Frits always enjoyed the campaign trail, and this year he was especially gratified to be able to thank in person all those people who had sent him cards and prayers and mementos while he was at Henry Ford Hospital in Detroit. His dedication and sincerity, as well as his hard work within the legislature itself, won him reelection once again. The Fourth Legislature would still not give Crucians equal representation compared to the St. Thomas district, but with the 1960 election and thereafter, they would hold on to five seats until reapportionment was finally approved in Congress.

Nationally, young, dynamic John F. Kennedy of Massachusetts was elected to the White House. Kennedy had campaigned for domestic reforms, which he called the "New Frontier." He promised tax reforms, federal aid to education, medical care for elderly through Social Security programs, and extended civil rights. At the age of forty–three, the youngest man to become president, Kennedy was a strong Democratic party man. He appointed longtime V.I. Democratic national committeeman Ralph M.

Paiewonsky to be governor of the Virgin Islands. All of the territory's longtime supporters in Congress won reelection, and the possibilities for development seemed endless. With Paiewonsky, the territory not only had a savvy national player, but a local man with close ties to the business community in St. Thomas and the politicians of Savan. In response to national directives to get the territory's political act together, Governor Paiewonsky sent down and, in June 1961, the legislature passed, act 696 creating a new election code which would provide recognition and management of political parties and provide for public primary elections. A law firm was authorized to develop the document. Despite violent objections, mainly to public primaries, this document moved swiftly as Title 18 was adopted in February 1963. Under Kennedy's call, the V.I. legislature also passed the first civil rights act banning segregation and discrimination for reasons of race, creed, color or national origin, some three and a half years before the U.S. Congress would do so.

Members of a special committee on the organic act met at the White House in 1965 (L–R): Earle Ottley, Aubrey Anduze, unidentified aide, Theovald Moorehead, Ron DeLugo, Governor Ralph Paiewonsky, Frits Lawaetz

— Chapter Thirty–Six —

The Move to Industrialization

Two of the biggest changes to the territory came early in Frits's political career. After the military left St. Croix, politicians in Washington played with several ideas about developing the federal properties by the airport. They encouraged industrial development. In January 1962, during the term of Governor Ralph Paiewonsky, Leo Harvey promised to build an alumina plant on some of the land just east of the airport and to spend $3 million to dredge a ship channel, if the government would give him the 750 acres and award large tax subsidies. There was a promise of industrial jobs for locals, but this seemed suspicious since St. Croix was already importing thousands of aliens to fill jobs. The deal and the name of the company involved were kept rather quiet; the press could get little information. Public hearings were demanded, not because everyone was opposed to the idea, but because they wanted to know what was being proposed. When the hearing was finally held, businessmen attending were not allowed to put questions through an attorney or make their opposition known for the record. Opponents were declared "racist."

It soon was learned that the hearing was a joke, for the Unity majority had already confirmed the governor's contract with the alumina company in a secret session on 20 February 1962. When the compact was sent to the legislature, senators were given the agreement to vote up or down, no changes allowed. Frits strongly objected to the land giveaway to an unknown company. He urged the governor to buy all of the federal lands instead. Talks held at

Government House in St. Thomas, grew heated and the proponents accused Frits, the only white in the legislature, of racial bias. "They said I was against it, because I was trying to keep the poor little black man down and from good jobs. But I objected to no input first, and now the deal is written and we [in the legislature] can't change a comma." As the debate raged, Frits realized that his opponents were using the issue to foster racial friction, and he determined to not give them fodder for the idea. He spoke on the floor of the legislature of why he should vote against the Harvey deal, "but in hopes it may do some good for the people, I did vote for the bill and it passed."

"Leo Harvey and I became good friends after all that," Frits said. "Eventually he invested $50 million in the alumina plant, because it was under the stars and stripes of the American flag. Guyana lost out to us because of that, although Harvey did bring in some of his bauxite from there." But the action taken by the governor and the Unity majority was considered by many to be undemocratic. Opponents were less happy as a total of 1,200 acres went to Harvey for free, and the government assumed the costs of keeping its three–mile long boat channel constantly dredged. Jobs were created and filled by hundred of workers from the southern states and down–island, as there was a constant shortage of skilled labor on St. Croix. Lawsuits failed, and the prediction that the alumina refinery would spoil the south shore and pollute the island eventually proved too true.

When Leon Hess came down to the island in 1965 to investigate the possibility of opening an oil refinery, the legislature was handled a lot more tactfully. Hess was a hard working oil truck driver who developed his business into a mega–refinery operation in the 1950s. With the possibility of gaining a foothold at the crossroads of the shipping world, Hess carefully and politely made his offer to the governor, and the senators were invited to come to New Jersey to see how he operated his plants there. Frits was one of the five members who traveled to Perth Amboy in the spring of 1965. He was deeply impressed by the Hess operation, the cleanliness of every single piece of equipment, the white–painted structures and of the plant itself. "One of our people was up there working," Frits said, "Eric Nielsen, and he spoke well of Hess." Frits was told that, after a driver for Hess had been killed in a truck accident, Hess paid for the son's education. Although the refinery had no liability in the man's death, Hess was very loyal to his employees. Leon Hess told the visiting V.I. legislators that he didn't want to be in a community "where you don't want me." Frits retorted that Mr. Hess was passing the buck back to them, but he thought it gave stature to the man who felt that way. Frits recalls that he thought it would change the island to bring such a big plant but that two plants would be better for the labor market than one.

The visiting senators took Hess up on his offer to drive them around to competitive plants which were filthy and noisy operations. It was a shrewd strategic move and Frits appreciated the wisdom of it. Frits told Leon Hess, after thinking about it overnight, that he could see the good possibility but that any deal had to be legislated, not rammed down their throats by Government House; Hess agreed. A very fair agreement between Hess Oil and the Virgin Islands government was hammered out and passed in September. In order to avoid the problems Harvey ran into looking for skilled personnel to build and operate the alumina plant, Hess was required, among other things, to set up a training school.

Sadly, with both Harvey and Hess, local people were not only unskilled in most areas of the refinery work but unwilling to work. The Hess training school was set up first, but only one indigenous islander was in the first graduating class of forty–five trainees. Down–island men and women who had experience with refineries rushed to claim the jobs which paid triple the rates obtainable in the rest of the private sector. Other workers were brought in from the states to make up for the deficit in local interest. New housing, school seats and hospital beds were needed for the booming economy and for the growing population. Hess trained for ten years. Few locals ever entered the classes.

— Chapter Thirty–Seven —

Progress

Between 1960 and 1970, as provisions made by the first three legislatures matured, the population more than doubled from 33,425 to 75,151. It would be almost tripled by 1975. Many migrated from the states, even more came up from the Lesser Antilles. The infrastructure put into place with the $10 million gained under Governor Harwood was stretched far beyond expectations. In January 1963, in order to handle the massive amount of work, the legislature's opening day was moved from mid–April back to the second Monday in January of each year; but sessions would still commence at 2:00 P.M. Sessions were to run for sixty days. The new legislative rules provided, for the first time, for individual offices and staff in both St. John and St. Croix. Space was rented in a two–story office building on Contentment Road just outside the western entry to Christiansted.

Meanwhile, sugar cane farming, the mainstay of the island of St. Croix since the earliest known settlements of the 1630s, was becoming harder to maintain because of minimum wage laws and the low prices paid by VICORP to the sugar cane growers. Over the years Frits had successfully worked for passage of many benefits for small growers. In 1959 the legislature had provided subsidy payments of fifty dollars for each new acre planted in cane and one dollar for each ton of cane delivered to the factory, to bridge the gap between VICORP payments and real costs. The original maximum subsidy was set at $3,500 per grower; this was later reduced to $2,000. The subsidy ceiling for new cane acreage remained at a maximum of thirty acres.

Another revolving fund for farmers and fishermen was set up in 1961 to help combat the rise in the cost of living, with interest a maximum of four percent. These special funds were renewed again and again to help farmers survive. When cutting amounts paid for cane was thwarted, VICORP set up a wage scale for their workers that was lower than that set by the legislature. The legislature had to petition Congress to make VICORP use the V.I. wage scale. In 1962 $30,000 was appropriated to the Special Conservation Fund to match USDA programs for local projects; this provided awards of up to $5,000 per person to help farmers meet plant, soil, and water conservation practices endorsed locally and federally. Dams had been built on St. Croix, water catchments dotted the hillsides in St. Thomas, and when droughts came, help was made available. These hard won programs did not, however, stop the decline in farming, because it seemed that VICORP wanted to go out of operation and Governor Paiewonsky actively worked for its demise.

Frits says, concerning VICORP, that Ward Canaday and Ralph Paiewonsky had serious differences. Some differences surely arose from the amount of power Canaday wielded on the board of VICORP, a board which Paiewonsky, as governor, thought was his to direct. Canaday was the largest landholder in the territory — he owned about four thousand acres and leased more. And Canaday, appointed by the president of the United States, held a seat on the VICORP board of directors specifically reserved for a sugar cane grower. By choice or chicanery, Canaday was absent when the vote about closing Bethlehem was held. As part of their argument that VICORP was unprofitable, VICORP accountants used depreciation of equipment and structures to show the federal project was losing money in operations. Frits and other farmers thought that, when an agency is federally organized and operated and pays no tax, it should not use depreciation to factor its profit or loss.

Daily News reporter, Bill Steif, noted that, although the price of sugar was the highest ever in forty years, and the V.I. agricultural department reported that oranges would not grow satisfactorily on St. Croix, Governor Paiewonsky pushed for closure and leasing of the land to National Bulk Carriers, a firm owned by New York shipping magnate Daniel K. Ludwig. It was said that Ludwig's firm intended to mix its Panama–produced juice with St. Croix orange juice and ship it into the United States, avoiding tariffs as a "made in the USA" product. The factory, Paiewonsky said, would invest more than $12 million and employ 150 workers, twice that of VICORP. In the *Legislative Record* for 5 October 1962, his fifty–fifth birthday, Frits went on record saying,

> Mr. President, I am one among thousands of people in the Virgin Islands who are very shocked to hear that the governor of the Virgin Islands got up on the floor of the last Board of Directors of the Virgin Islands Corporation meeting and made a motion to stop the sugar cane operation in St. Croix especially after the 1963 crop. Up to that day, there were people in St. Croix planting cane that could not be harvested before 1964. At the last Board of Directors meeting this same problem had come up, and as I recall, the people were told that they would have five years to liquidate the company and would be given sufficient time to recover any investment they might have made in sugar cane. Many people feel that the loss of $100,000 in the [VICORP] operation of cane is a lot of money. But you must remember that this industry turns over about $2 million in the run of a year — for a crop like the last one we had....I don't know where Mr. Alexander got the figure of $40,000 [paid to growers], but I can assure you that the small growers collect [much more].
>
> Mr. President, a $2 million operation of an industry revolves in the community about 8 to 10 times, and that would mean that that $2 million changes hands about 8 times before it disintegrates. I would make a recommendation that we ask Congress to continue the operation of the Virgin Islands Corporation as long as the charter is in effect, and I think that is until 1969.

> We are spending billions of dollars in the United States on foreign aid, giving a lot to Communistic countries and here we bring in from the neighboring islands people who are all, I would say, 100 percent pro–American, 700 to 800 people to carry on the operations of this industry, plus maybe about 400 to 500 native people. They said that the intent for the [original] setting up of the Corporation does not operate anymore. That is not true. If VICORP was to stop operating tomorrow, you will have about 400 native people out of work.
>
> I also think that the committee that we have in this legislature to look into the operations of VICORP should be reactivated and as soon as possible investigate some of these figures that we are hearing about and which to me seem to be fantastic. Because I heard that they are claiming that they are losing half a million dollars; and I question that. And I question whether we will spend a million dollars to repair the mill....I think this is a most serious matter, because this is an industry that has kept my island alive for 200 years. And all of a sudden, without asking the advice of the people who know a little about it, the Governor goes and makes a motion...to liquidate it within a year.

On 8 February 1962, opening day of a special session, the legislature passed a resolution confirming the governor's intention to accept the responsibility for VICORP property and spend $10 million over the next ten years to operate the facilities. What was not known at this time was that the $10 million would be used for buying VICORP's two district power plants, not running the sugar cane factory. With rumors running rampant, in February 1963, at Paiewonsky's urging, the Unity–dominated legislature recommended the government match the highest bid on the St. Croix VICORP properties of 1,700 acres in sugar cane, "in order to keep sugar cane farming alive." Two days later the governor and V.I. Citrus (a subsidiary of National Bulk Carriers) signed a memorandum of agreement for a contract–and–lease to begin a $20 million project on the same 1,700 acres. The memo suggested that growers establish cooperatives and that V.I. Citrus Company would sell them trees "without profit." Ironically, the government failed to outbid Lawrence Harvey (brother of Leo Harvey) of Harvey Alumina on the VICORP lands. The Panama connection failed, presumably because National Bulk Carriers would have to buy the land from Harvey, not lease it at low price.

Despite the wishes of St. Croix farmers, on 14 March 1963 Resolution 235 was passed in support of the intention of the government to terminate the sugar mill operation by 30 June 1963. Bethlehem was declared uneconomical: "the cultivation of sugar cane is, at best, an activity of dubious economic rationality in the USVI." Certainly not the sentiments of the five hundred growers and seventy–five mill workers who were being thrown out of work. Originally the government intended to let the delivery of the 1964, 1965, and 1966 crops be shipped away for grinding, since one can't stop the canes from growing over their life span of three–to–five years. But as it happened, Harvey refused to sell the land but agreed to operate the Bethlehem mill, and so it remained open until June 1966 when, by agreement, Frits Lawaetz of Annaly Farms, with its three hundred acres — the largest sugar cane grower on the island — delivered the last load of sugar cane for processing. The engine of the last tractor train was buried under a massive blanket of native flowers; Frits was not sure if it should be a day of celebration or a day of sadness. Crucian voters have not forgotten nor easily forgiven St. Thomas politicians for those actions which reeked of complicity and deal–making. The vote to close VICORP lost them many farming and factory jobs and prime water marshes, although it opened the island up for heavy industrial development through the approval of the Harvey Alumina Company. The people whose jobs were lost were not able to compete for refinery jobs except at the lowest of entry levels, presuming they could read and write.

As a pacifier for farmers, act 1049 authorized low–cost transportation for other agricultural products shipped by sea or air, including fruits, vegetables, poultry and poultry products, cattle, milk and dairy products, and fish. But the twentieth century had

The last train of sugar cane from Upper Love, May 1966.
L–R; Amy, Manolin, John, Alfred and Frits.

been a dry one, and the failure to provide constant clean water for farmers meant there was little or no surplus of fruits and vegetables, poultry or livestock to be shipped. Kai Lawaetz was actively farming, and while he had lettuce and pineapples he sent to St. Thomas, he often was the only produce shipper. It would not be until the late 1980s that St. Croix produced enough milk to include St. Thomas on a regular shipping schedule.

As for Ward Canaday, seventy–seven years old in the mid–1960s, he worked up an agreement to donate 4,200 acres of his cattle lands to Harvard and Bryn Mawr, his and his wife's alma maters, with the provision that they sell them to Laurence and David Rockefeller. The colleges benefited with the addition of dormitories at Harvard and a new library for Bryn Mawr, built from the proceeds of the sale. The Rockefeller brothers planned to build a hotel and retirement community with a first–class golf course (Fountain Valley) on some of the land. Canaday retained thirty–four acres of Estate Annaly and sixty–four acres at Estate Blue Mountain for his personal use and leased back all but 330 acres from the Rockefellers to continue running his beloved Annaly Farms.

In August 1964, Frits was able to get a resolution passed which urged that heads of families and others left bereft of sugar cane work and with no other employable skills be absorbed into government service and/or be part of newly created public works programs and given special consideration for government controlled housing.

— Chapter Thirty–Eight —

Ups and Downs

The first $1.5 million to buy the power plants from VICORP was authorized the summer of 1963. The following summer the Virgin Islands Water and Power Authority, authorized by Interior, was created as a separate and distinct authority with the right to issue bonds of its own. Approval also was given for the government to buy "Subbase" as surplus Marine Corps war property and to buy the St. Thomas airport from VICORP. Delay on the work of developing the St. Thomas airport began when Governor Paiewonsky wanted it moved to the east end of the island so his beloved college would not have to cope with the noise of aircraft. The Unity faction passed an act authorizing him to buy two hundred acres at east end; public opinion shot down the idea.

Even before the closure of Bethlehem, owners began subdividing their sugar cane lands for resale. In response to evictions of tenants from estate villages, Frits and other senators moved in 1961 to have the governor make land available at Annaberg and Profit and Spanish Town for those unfortunate folks. The government as usual was slow to get moving, and many families began building their own units by hand without titles. The biggest evictions came to families living at Strawberry Hill and Baron Spot Estate. Some families used the stones thrown down by bulldozers to rebuild elsewhere. Others weren't so fortunate. Frits became personally involved to make sure Profit lands were parceled out as mandated in 1961. In March 1963 the legislature added in the building of a day care center, playground and a community center; Profit exists today because of Frits's concern for his fellow farmers, although this new "village" would take years to complete. In 1965 a hostile committee held up distribution of land to the lessees. For the patient people in Profit, it was not until January 1970 that act 2613 authorized $100,000 to be used to build turnkey housing for the predominantly Hispanic residents; a few weeks later water, sewers, roads and sidewalks were approved. (Recreational lights were also passed but never installed.) As the scheduled end of cane production came closer, more estates began closing their villages in order to partition and develop the properties for uses other than farming; evictions occurred in Prosperity, William, Lower Love, Coble, and Old Castle Coakley. By April 1967, much more housing was needed and ten acres were set aside for a project at Kings Hill, now called Aureo Diaz Heights. Sion Farm turnkey project was authorized for moderate–income families in 1968.

Annaly Farms kept its employees going despite the end of sugar refining. Natalio Ponce, Pollo, and Manolin kept operating the field tractors between 1960 and 1980, and their children found work in the operation as well. Natalio's son is now the chief butcher, while John Bryan, another operator who worked with Annaly Farms from 1954 until 1995, is father of the chief cashier at the Estate Upper Love operation. As compensation for his Jeep accident, Ward Canaday settled seventy acres of pasture land at Estate Upper Love on Frits, part of which now houses the abattoir and cooler. One of the longest serving leaders at Annaly was Alfonzo "Wyson" Correa, who followed in his father's footsteps to become top cowboy and now has more than fifty years on the range. It was only in 1998 that Wyson agreed to work just part time. Tonio Bermudez, a third generation cowboy, is now the top cowboy for Annaly Farms. And in his turn, Tonio is providing apprenticeship training for a new generation of cowboys.

Frits recalls getting sick during a legislative session in St. Thomas. He thought it was a recurrence of malaria, which he had in his system since childhood, but after failing to respond to treatment, he had to call for medical attention. Dr. Rice, who had served in Africa for many years, suspected an elephantiasis attack and ordered new blood tests at 10:00 in the evening. When asked why, he replied that the filariasis worms were only active in the blood late at night. Sure enough, worms were found, and, thanks to early detection, Frits was cured by a few shots of a drug produced by Ligget Pharmaceutical from plants collected by Frits's old friend, Harry Beatty, and sent to Liggett by Ward Canady. It was a real wonder drug to islanders, but, economically insignificant to Liggett, it would not have been manufactured had it not been for Canady's insistence. This drug was as important to Virgin Islanders as the many long–term jobs Canady created in St. Croix.

Frits was able, through his connections in Washington as a V.I. senator and through his personal connection to Ward Canaday to get a one hundred percent federally funded program extended to the Virgin Islands to prevent and then eradicate brucellosis, a bacterial infection which can produce spontaneous abortions in cattle and recurrent fever and joint pain in humans. Funding for the V.I. program also included vaccinations for hog cholera. With these problems erased, Virgin Islands farmers could look forward in the near future to exporting livestock and meat products. Annaly's Senepol breed would be well received as an export, according to a letter from internationally–regarded tropical–farming expert Dicky Frampton of the Department of Science and Agriculture, Barbados, who wrote that he wanted to buy some of their Senepols and wanted them shipped at the same time Frits would be sending cattle to Venezuela. Frampton said, "I regard your Senepol herd as one of the greatest contributions to the building up of a first class beef business in this part of the world, and even further afield."

Hans returned, as agreed, to help with Annaly Farms after his tour with the Air Force ended in 1964. First based in Texas, then in Charleston, South Carolina, he spent some of his time in service playing baseball. By the end of 1961 he was transferred to Ramey

Air Force Base in Puerto Rico, where it was easier for him to rent a Cessna and get home to Annaly on weekends. Hans met Judith Riggs of Chicago there, a teacher at the base school, whom he described to Frits and Bodil as "the most wonderful girl in the world." In March 1962 they were married. After his return home, Hans signed papers naming him an equal partner in Annaly Farms, along with his father and Ward Canaday. The new partnership leased 4,200 acres of pasture land from the Rockefeller brothers, had 1,500 head of cattle and grew 300 acres of sugar cane. It was agreed that Canaday would be the absentee partner; Frits would continue his work in the legislature and handle paperwork for the farm. Hans would run the day–to–day operation. Hans supplemented the usual cattle feed with imported cotton seed meal and fourteen percent protein feed. This helped get young cattle ready for slaughter sooner.

Hans returned at a time when it seemed that St. Croix would finally begin to share in the prosperity that St. Thomas had been experiencing. Hopes ran high, and friends and family members abroad were written and told about the possibilities. The actual construction of the Hess Oil refinery was expected to have a four–fold multiplier effect. The de Chabert family, after selling Leon Hess their family land, began planning the Sunny Isle Shopping Center. La Reine Shopping Center with a bowling alley started construction, and transplanted continental residents collected money to build the Island Center for the Performing Arts. Over at Howard Wall's Estate at Cane Garden, young Caroline came home with her husband, Mario Gasperi, to take over Castle Nugent's cattle operations. Enrico Gasperi and his wife came in from Italy to help in 1966. An entirely new generation began taking over; there were demands for new schools, new homes, and the cost of living went ever higher. After Hess won the import allocation of 15,000 barrels per day per year into the United States District I through IV from the Department of the Interior, islanders realized exactly how much the refinery would bring in besides the jobs and spin–off industries. The quota meant $7,500 per day in royalties to the V.I., all going into the Conservation Fund to be used for air and water pollution control, sewage treatment systems and facilities, parks, recreation, preservation and beautification. The potential impact was stunning. With the quota in hand, the V.I. legislature passed Act 2093, which required Hess to employ a minimum of five hundred people, in addition to construction people, within thirty–six months, and to invest an additional investment of $70 million within a year and $30 million more within the next three years.

The legislature began a concerted drive to end the brain drain and bring home islanders to fill those jobs. Sharing in the good times, Annaly Farms had ten to fifteen young cattle going to slaughter every Monday and was in the meat business delivering beef right to the grocery stores. Hans soon set up his own wholesale outlet, Annaly Farms Market at Upper Love, where it still sells Senepol beef and other food products.

— Chapter Thirty–Nine —

Party Battles

The new election code of 1963, introduced and rammed through by the Unity party majority members, took power out of the hands of local branches of the national parties by establishing public primaries and giving any person the right to register with a party regardless of his or her personal views. Further, nominations under the party banner were to be done by petition. Trouble began immediately.

The Democratic party registered its affiliation to the national party with the newly created supervisor of elections on 19 April 1963. The Unity party, which had no national affiliation, voted to change their name to the Democratic party of the Virgin Islands, identical to the real Democrats. They took their party registration to the new supervisor on 1 May, the final day for filing. Objecting, the "real Democrats" requested a hearing, which Henrita Todman, supervisor of elections, denied. After refusing twice to consider the matter, Todman was named in a law suit filed by the real or "Donkey" Democrats. In district court the case was heard by Judge Walter A. "Roy" Gordon, former governor of the Virgin Islands, who had been sorely abused by the Unity party during his term in office, both through the media and on the floor of the legislature. In retaliation for Ottley's harassment at the time, Gordon had ordered all government advertisements removed from the *Home Journal,* a newspaper owned by Ottley.

Judge Gordon decided in favor of the Donkey Democrats, stating the Unity party members had attempted a takeover in a fraudulent scheme. He ordered Todman to strike the Unity members from the Democratic territorial committee and certify only those who were Donkey Democrats. The defeated group, using their Unity party symbol, calling themselves "Mortar and Pestle" Democrats, and led by Ralph Paiewonsky, previously the Democratic national committeeman, appealed and won a stay of Judge Gordon's order until the case could be heard by the U. S. Third Circuit Court.

When the Mortar and Pestle group held rallies and printed literature with the sponsor given as the "St. John Democratic Club," this too went to court, and the "Mortar and Pestle" group was ordered by the court to cease using the word "Democratic" in any further activities until the case was resolved.

The delay in having the case heard by the Third Circuit Court caused more trouble. Todman certified that sixteen Mortar and Pestle members and six Donkey members had been elected to the new territorial committee. The Donkey members refused to recognize the others at the first meeting; with the power of the majority, Mortar and Pestle members replaced them with six members of their group who had lost in the elections. This led to both factions, Donkey and Mortar and Pestle, sending delegates to the Democratic National Convention in Atlantic City in August 1964.

The Donkeys, led by the elected national committeeman Ron DeLugo and national committeewoman Lucinda Millin and Joe Alexander, state chairman for the past twenty–five years, included Frits (who, upon loss of the legal battle, did not go), as well as Senator Doward and Senator Moorehead, the then Government Secretary Cyril King, former Government Secretary Daniel Ambrose, and presidents of the local Democratic clubs.

The Mortar and Pestle faction was led by Governor Ralph Paiewonsky. In total control of the Democratic territorial committee and the governorship, Mortar and Pestle members were seated at the convention.

The Third Circuit Court overturned Judge Gordon's decision in November, finding the fight to be local and political and outside the court's jurisdiction. Control of the Democratic party by "Unicrats" (Unity party members) would stand. Earle Ottley said in his book, *Trials and Triumphs*, some of the Unity people hoped that once they controlled the Democratic party opponents would switch to become Republicans and thus create a real two–party system, as pushed by the House Interior and Insular Affairs Committee. Underestimating Democratic allegiance to party principles, Ottley said, "We [Unity members] were mistaken." When the old Donkey Democrats were unable to get a slate signed by the territorial committee, they ran as independent candidates under Donkey symbols.

Frits was appalled and disgusted at the blatant takeover and open intention of Earle Ottley and Ralph Paiewonsky to run government between themselves from St. Thomas, with consessions thrown occasionally to Frits and Lucinda Millin whom Ottley also liked. For ten years Frits had specifically declined to align with any party because of the cronyism tactics and favoritism he had seen. Frits firmly believed that the elected senators were there to work for the betterment of all of the people, not for personal gain or prestige. He found the Unity dictatorship unacceptable. A conservative champion of the workers, Frits signed up with the Donkey Democrats and jumped into the fray as a Donkey Democrat party man.

For the 1964 election, Ottley wanted a clear, dedicated majority beholden to him only and decided his old allies, Walter Hodge and Candido Guadelupe, had to go. Randall "Doc" James and Patrick Williams agreed to run and were chosen to run against them. Earle Ottley let his people in St. Thomas know that they could skip voting for himself and Johnny Maduro because they had enough votes and that they should concentrate on getting James and Williams of St. Croix voted into two of the at large seats. The tactic worked: Williams and James polled more votes in St. Thomas than they garnered at home. Williams was dropped by the Unicrats two years later in favor of Aureo Diaz and the Puerto Rican vote, although Doc James would serve a total of four two–year terms before returning to his radio show and medical practice full time. Ottley stated in *Trials and Triumphs* that Williams was paid for his agreement to drop out of the race with the post of executive director in the legislature and ever since, as promised by Ottley, he has been assigned various traveling board positions.

The 1964 campaign year was extraordinary for its dirty tricks and sabotage. At one point Frits's home was called and Bodil told that one of her family members had been taken to hospital "as he deserved." It was many desperate hours before she found out that all the brothers, sons and nephews scattered around the island, as well as in the states, were well and safe. But as Frits announced loudly at the next rally, "Whoever was responsible needs to stop, because, while I am strong like a bull and can take any of you on, my family is not running in this race and you have no right to involve them or bring them to danger." When the police department assigned him protection, he refused. When the officer followed him to church, Frits put his artificial foot down smartly and refused to be protected while at worship. He said, "The House of God is a sanctuary, and if I cannot be at peace here, then there is no freedom for anyone." The dirty tricks continued and the power battle waged on for years. The Mortar and Pestle group might have control of the party and the legislature, but it could not dominate St. Croix or St. John. To prevent coalition forming, a loyalty oath was passed but thrown out by the court, because it bound senators to party leaders and prohibited freedom of thought and action. It "tied up" senators, Judge Maris said, "like bunches of beets."

Election battles were over by early November. Frits did not talk about them with Mor as usual, because her attention was on her own mortality. She would be ninety–two the following March and was feeling frail. In the lull between elections and the January start–up of the legislature, Frits went down to Little La Grange most evenings to sit a little while with Mor and talk of life and why it was taking her so long to die of old age. Frits told her Jesus may need a lot more time to prepare room for her, because of her many good works and her long, loving friendships with everyone who crossed her path.

The family enjoyed their traditional Christmas Eve celebrations at Little La Grange; Kai's wife Irene, of French descent from St. Barth's, had mastered the many Danish treats for the family and was helped by Kai and their seven year old daughter, Suzanne. Anna was there; Frits and Bodil were there with young Fritsie; Hans and Judy brought two–year old Amy; Erik and Jenny came with Roy, Mona and David. The only ones missing were Bent and Sally, still in Panama, and Else, still in Denmark with her family. It was a perfect time after campaign chaos for Frits.

At the end of the year, on 30 December 1964, Frits's mother, Marie Lawaetz, died peacefully, happy to join her husband and two little girls who had preceded her. She was laid to rest beside Carl in the garden at Little La Grange. Her life had left sweet memories in many places.

Christmas 1965 Back row (l–r): Hans, Fritsie, Frits, Bent. Front row: Judy, Amy, Bodil, Jodie, Sally.

The next two years were, politically, as full of conflicts as before. The overthrow of the oath allowed Donkeys to run with Republicans in 1966 under the banner of Victory 66, choosing the eagle as their coalition symbol. This was the first year voters would elect fifteen members to the legislature. Mortar and Pestle Democrats went out to scour the bushes for acceptable and pliable candidates to add to their field. When the votes were counted, Mortar and Pestle had won all four at large seats and five in St. Thomas; the coalition won all of St. Croix and the one St. John seat for a total of five. Among the losers were Donkey partisans Ron DeLugo and Bertha Boschulte. Following the debacle, at the last special session of the Sixth Legislature, Johnny Maduro and Earle Ottley offered "eulogies." Frits countered with remarks that "Ron's voice has been heard here and in Washington, and it has always been a voice for the people." On his own behalf, DeLugo said the words were kind, but he was too young to write his memoirs.

Frits had campaigned harder in 1966 against the Mortar and Pestle domination than he ever had. He bought time on television to say,

> There is no doubt in my mind that if the Unicrats get control of the Legislature...they will amend the election code so that all electors may vote for all fifteen candidates in the 1968 election, thereby eliminating the voice of all minorities and giving them complete dictatorship, which has always been their aim. The intent of the governor and majority senators to place the people...under the domain of dictatorship controlled by the political bosses in St. Thomas is very clear.

Frits warned the voters that, if they did not elect honest and courageous men and women to defend the rights of the people of St. Croix, the island would be controlled and annexed to St. Thomas as Buck Island is to St. Croix today. He branded a new scheme illegal. Passed at special session, the scheme allowed residents of the other district to vote in St. Croix's primary, although they could not vote for them in the general election. "Who condones this invasion of St. Croix candidates to be elected by St. Thomas, but Crucians who have become puppets to unscrupulous men: How long, how long, will you be traitors to our beloved St. Croix?"

The battle still raged at the beginning of 1968. Then in March, the elected governor bill passed Congress. The month preceding passage, John M. Bailey, chairman of the Democratic national committee sent Dan Rostenkowski, a congressman representing the district of Chicago, to the islands to unite the warring factions. He ordered unification and appointed a committee to draw up a plan. With the right to elect a governor and a non–voting representative to Congress looming, there had to be an end to Democratic party fighting. Much of the friction was between the two top men in the executive branch, Ralph Paiewonsky and Cyril King.

Given the national political scene, no one in Washington had any more time to spend on the little territory. Eugene McCarthy was challenging President Lyndon Johnson. Although McCarthy's popular support finally forced Johnson out of the race, Hubert Humphrey was nominated over McCarthy at the Democratic National Convention. In the general election, Humphrey, for whom Government Secretary Cyril King once worked, won the popular vote, but Nixon had the majority of the electoral college. The Democrats' eight–year lock on the White House was over.

Cyril King was one who refused to cooperate with the direct orders from Washington. At public meetings in May, where party members of the clubs would vote, senators Augustin Doward and Frits Lawaetz and former Senator Ron DeLugo stated their reasons for supporting the merger. Santiago Garcia, a well respected Puerto Rican businessman, also spoke eloquently in favor of ending the rift. In Frederiksted the meeting fell into chaos when the club president, Alexander Moorhead Jr., said, before King could give his viewpoint, that only paid members of the club could vote on the question. When that condition was challenged as unprecedented and a list of paid members was not even available, Moorhead refused to be moved. After much ruckus, Moorhead resigned immediately. The *Home Journal* reported that, following his resignation, Moorhead's mother announced that the club owed her nearly a year's rent on the headquarters and she wanted payment without delay. Vice President Frances "Bea" Christensen, mother–

in–law to Frits's brother Erik, had endorsed the merger and rescheduled a meeting for the next week. Cyril King told Frits that he escaped a severe tongue–lashing that night over his position, but Frits responded that he was ready to go on the rostrum anytime to face the people. King's ally, Steve O'Reilly, promised to take Frits's seat at the next election. Later on, Earle Ottley, Ron DeLugo, Frits and some others sat down together to work out a compromise with Cyril King. Frits told Cyril King that he had been put into the position of government secretary by a Democratic president and should stay loyal, stay with the party and and work within it, but Cyril was stubborn and broke away to form the Independent Citizens Movement to support his own run for governor. Many residents, tired of the chaos and perceived cronyism broke away as well. When the unified Democrats ran in 1968, all of them were reelected; it was the first fifteen–person legislature. Ironically Earle and Frits were to agree that having a fifteen–person majority wasn't good either; the legislature needed a majority–minority split to provide opposing viewpoints. Furthermore, a much more serious problem was that Earle held the controlling reins and the power remained fixed firmly in St. Thomas.

— Chapter Forty —

The First Election for Governor

The newly inaugurated Republican president, Richard Nixon, accepted Governor Paiewonsky's resignation on 7 February 1969 and gave him five days to vacate Government House in St. Thomas. Because Nixon named no successor, Government Secretary Cyril King moved up to become acting governor of the Virgin Islands on 13 February.

King, who had aspired to the governorship since John Kennedy won nomination to the presidency in 1960, initiated a flurry of projects in order to demonstrate to President Nixon his ability to be governor. Apparently King even offered to join the Republican party, so that he might be appointed to that office. But local Republicans reacted in outrage and demanded consideration for one of their own. Peter Bove, the federally appointed V.I. comptroller general, was recommended to the president and then appointed.

Bove, a white man from Vermont and federally appointed, was well received, despite the mounting local climate pitting black against white. However, Bove, due to ill health, withdrew his name during the congressional hearings. Lacking Bove, who had been a popular choice, the Republicans turned to former health commissioner, Melvin Evans, Frits's personal physician, who switched over from the Democratic party in order to be appointed by the U.S.

president. He was confirmed by the U.S. Senate and sworn in on 1 July 1969.

Out of work, Cyril King moved to St. Croix and spent his time crafting the new Independent Citizens Movement (ICM) for disgruntled Democrats.

In 1968, the Congress at last passed legislation that would allow Virgin Islanders to elect their own governor, and they would do so for the first time in November 1970.

It was clear Evans would run as the Republican candidate, and the Republican party sent down one of their top managers to handle his campaign. It also was clear early on that Cyril King would run for the post as head of the new ICM party.

But by the sheer number of members, the Democrats expected their party to win the governor's seat in the 1970 election, and they looked for a candidate who could unify the Unicrats and the Donkeys, after Paiewonsky wisely declared he was not a candidate.

Paiewonsky might have won. During his term the number of persons on the government payroll had shot sky high. The budget, $8 million when Paiewonsky was confirmed, had multiplied six times over, to $48.9 million. The college, Paiewonsky's pet project was getting near to $2 million, and at the stroke of midnight, as Paiewonsky was leaving Government House, the chairmanship of the college's Board of Directors was assured for Ralph Paiewonsky by his cohort, Earle B. Ottley. Funds were becoming very tight, however, and a long–term downturn loomed. By stepping back at this time, Paiewonsky assured himself a place in history: during his tenure, there had been continual economic advance and no recession — never mind the loss of farm jobs and the severe increase in industry–caused air and water pollution in St. Croix.

Ottley immortalized Paiewonsky in the *Legislative Record* for "better homes, more jobs, increased health and social services, vastly improved education...a better life and higher standard of living for all of our people." That too was true. It was also true that during his eight–year watch, juvenile delinquency rose to plague the population and drug problems required special legislation.

With Paiewonsky out as a candidate, Earle Ottley's choice was Alexander A. Farrelly, a well respected attorney, because, though Farrelly was a resident of St. Thomas for most of his adult life, he was born in St. Croix. Farrelly was serving his second term in the Virgin Islands legislature when Ottley decided he had more chance to win Crucian votes away from Dr. Evans than long–term senator John Maduro.

Ottley knew his party needed the Puerto Rican vote as well, so he also pledged Democratic support for his two legislative choices in St. Croix, Santiago Garcia and Jose Figueroa. Coupled with his longstanding support of Frits, Doc James and Arnold "Morty" Golden, that left one seat for the rest of the Democratic candidates to fight for. Ottley's actions preceded the local Democratic convention and angered some Democrats. Paiewonsky chose to back his former attorney general, Francisco "Kiko" Corneiro, as the party's candidate for governor, and he was joined by campaign workers who wanted Maduro. Abandonment of faithful Democratic candidates for the legislature in St. Croix by Ottley severely drained the pool of campaign workers dedicated to the party effort, as David Hamilton filed to run independently, and Ruby Rouss attacked the Democrats and Farrelly for lack of loyalty throughout the rest of the campaign. After the convention, Francisco Corneiro from St. Thomas challenged Farrelly in the primary election. Though Corneiro lost, he pulled away the votes of many staunch old Unicrats.

All three candidates (Melvin Evans under the Republican banner, Cyril King for the ICM, and Alexander Farrelly for the Democrats) encountered the black versus white issue.

A black power movement actually gathered enough strength to command two–hours of television time in June 1970. Frits participated in the televised black power dialogue, where Alton Adams, Sr., long associated with the tourism industry, called the tourism that islanders had created a monstrosity. Governor Evans said he was surprised by the depth of feeling presented, while the former governor, Ralph Paiewonsky, said tourism was the fastest way to build an economic base for the people. It wasn't easy to encourage hotels and investment, but once it was done, Paiewonsky said, natives failed to reach out and make an effort.

Frits said that provisions in the charters of both Harvey Alumina and Hess Oil required the companies to hire native Virgin Island workers, if they are qualified, to fill at least seventy–five percent of the jobs, but few Virgin Islanders were enrolling in the free vocational training. Frits said he was sorry that the legislature's intention of bringing in jobs through tourism wasn't working out so far.

The acting president of CVI, Arthur Richards, told the audience that training programs for tourism had always failed for lack of interest. Valentine Penha, the Black Cultural Organization minister of education demanded to know why native participation was not required, why hotel owners were not required to build homes for workers, and why other paternalistic guarantees that had been thrown out with slavery were not required. Without question, islanders were not taking up the challenge; how to stimulate their interest to do so remains unanswered to this day.

Several years later the Virgin Islands Businessmen's Association (VIBA — a sort of black chamber of commerce) was formed. Neither group garnered long–term support. As Earle Ottley noted in his speech in 1969 calling for the merger of the Donkey and Unity Democrats, politicians had to stop whipping up fears about a white takeover, because "you cannot whip up hate in November and bottle it up in January" — an interesting lesson learned by the master craftsman of political tricks that had been used since the late 1950s to manipulate voters.

As the campaign rolled on, King, with his personal charisma and fiery accusations, attracted huge crowds. He even attacked Frits's records, which caused Frits to say, "Many of Mr. King's statements are false. Why Mr. King attacked me is amusing to say the least, as I have not declared myself a candidate for governor. He did not once mention what he planned to do for the good people....May I suggest that he think in terms of what good he can do, rather than be bitter."

Evans had the edge of incumbency, but the Democrats, at least, did not expect him to be a strong opponent. They were sadly mistaken. Evans won. The battles over the convention and again in the primary lost the Democrats the governorship, plus seats in the legislature. The Democratic candidate for governor came in third, and, from a fifteen–person majority in 1968, the Democrats lost all but six seats.

After eight terms in office, on St. Croix Frits came in eighth, losing by just thirty–four votes. Also gone were Democrats Randall James, Augustin Doward, Santiago Garcia, Morty Golden, and David Hamilton. Aureo Diaz had retired prior to the race. Every newly elected senator from St. Croix was a rookie to politics; three were Republicans, three were members of the ICM; just one was a Democrat, young Lew Muckle.

In St. Thomas Ariel Melchior and Virdin Brown, ICM men, were elected. Elroy Sprauve took over in St. John, another ICM man. The remaining five seats went to St. Thomas Democrats who provided the core of experience.

In all there were six Democrats, six ICM, and three Republicans. The tie in seats held by Democrats and members of the ICM would be broken by the Republicans.

On 11 November 1970 Frits wrote to his youngest son Fritsie at Stetson University in Florida,

> After sixteen years it seems that I am now a free man. As Mammie said: Well, I may have lost a senator but gained a husband. I have worked hard for this Island and can look every citizen in the eye, for I am not ashamed of any of the thousand decisions I had to make as their senator. At the time I made them, I did so, believing it was the best for my fellowmen....I can point my finger on so many projects and truthfully say, I played a part in this. The question then is why did I not get reelected? Three years ago I played an active part in merging the two factions of the Democratic Party....[but] the merger was not acceptable to many long term Democrats, who

> strongly resented the Unity Party Members registering as Democrats, and outvot[ing] the old guards at the Primary Election.

Frits told his son that the greater issue was to create a true two–party system, so that Congress would be comfortable and glad that the right to elect a governor had been extended to Virgin Islanders. It was never expected to further fractionalize the Democrats and create another party, the Independent Citizens Movement. He noted that many have not forgiven him for throwing his allegiance to the united Democratic party, but "history will bear me out, that I made the right decision." Frits turned his attention back to Annaly Farms.

— Chapter Forty–one —

The Turbulent Seventies

Bodil and Frits took their two oldest granddaughters with them to Denmark on the charter arranged by the Friends of Denmark in the summer of 1973. Bodil and Frits were charter members of the Friends, which traded visits with their counterparts in the Danish West Indian Society of Denmark. There were alternating two–week visits every four years. Amy, eleven, and Jodie, nearly eight, had a wonderful time seeing Tivoli Gardens and the colorful school marching bands in Copenhagen. They visited Otto's farm where Frits had worked summers and his father Carl had served several apprenticeships. While in Denmark Frits, in his official capacity as a member of the Virgin Islands Bicentennial Commission, met with members of the Danish West Indian Society and government officials to discuss the arrangements being made for the two hundredth anniversary of American Independence. The Danes would be taking a major part in the celebrations, and it was announced that Queen would come for Transfer Day observances.

That same year, Hans and Frits began buying Ward Canaday's shares in Annaly Farms. Hans began talking about operating a full butchery and cooler on the property at Upper Love, which Frits owned outright. The amount of beef now being sold out of Hans's house at River was astounding: they had contracts with the Department of Education and the Department of Health to provide beef to schools and hospitals. Hans felt he could do it better and earn a bigger profit by eliminating the middle man. Ward Canaday was

Annaly Farm partners Hans, Frits, Fritsie
While Frits continued his government service, work at Annaly Farms went on. Wyson is pictured below at the end of a long day.

not interested, although when Hans went to Selwyn Fleming for a loan to do it himself, Canaday was very annoyed. He felt that Hans should have asked him for the money. At the same time Hans and Frits were urging Baby Bull, young Fritsie, to leave the refinery and come work in the operation, as it was too much for Hans and Frits was too old to provide the manpower needed. Fritsie agreed and joined as a partner with fifteen percent of the shares. When the cooler was built, Hans got fifty percent ownership, and Frits and Fritsie got twenty–five percent each. With Baby Bull on board, Frits looked once again at elections in 1974.

Frits did not like being out of the legislature; he minded not being able to do things for the people of St. Croix. He thought the legislature had reacted rudely to Leon Hess's 1972 offer to build a new hospital on St. Croix when bids for a government hospital far outstripped available public funds. Because of senators' unbridled insults, the people lost out; it would be ten more years before one was built amid harsh criticism about quality of construction and overbuilding. As a private citizen, Frits had supported construction of the south shore power plant to attract new business to St. Croix. The island population now bulged at the seams, and new private–housing construction was going on at a rapid pace, particularly for Hess workers. Yet the economy in general was terrible, The refineries were accused of polluting the air and the water, and the pier in Frederiksted wasn't attracting as many cruise ships as had been hoped. There were eighty–six stops at St. Croix, compared to more than five hundred at St. Thomas. There were constant water shortages, skyrocketing prices, crime and unemployment. The school curriculums were not reflecting the needs of business, and Frits knew he could make a difference.

The biggest attraction in the 1974 race was for the governorship. Robert Maas had resigned as lieutenant governor in 1973, because he said Evans left him out of the decision–making process. Governor Evans had replaced him with a Democrat from the legislature (Athneil Ottley), which was one thing, but then he replaced Athneil Ottley with a Republican (Raymond Smith), and this had many Democrats crying foul. Down–island residents spoke vigorously against Evans, because of the alien sweep by the

Immigration and Naturalization Service. And many people did not like the fact that Val Washington, sent down by the Republican party in Washington, seemed to be making the decisions.

Still it took a while for the Democrats to come up with an enticing candidate. The Democratic convention in St. Croix left a sour taste in many mouths as favorite son, Aubrey Anduze, was dumped at the last minute by the power brokers of St. Thomas who backed Alexander Farrelly and Ruby Rouss. The primary battle, which Farrelly won two to one over Anduze, gave too much ammunition to the opposition. Farrelly never made it to the runoff, which was won by Cyril King as governor and political newcomer, Senator Juan Luis of St. Croix, as lieutenant governor.

In the general election, however, after four years out of office, Frits won reelection by the skin of his teeth. He was one of nine Democrats, seven of them from St. Thomas. The presidency went to Elmo Roebuck and Frits took back the chairmanship of the Public Works Committee which he had headed for most of his years in the legislature.

After King gave a stirring inaugural address (written by Frits's nephew by marriage, Peter Pardo de Zela, King's chief of staff and a great strategist), fiscal matters dominated the governorship of Cyril E. King. He vetoed bill after bill which appropriated funds with no valid source, laid off several hundred employees, and constantly withheld critical financial information from the legislature. Few days passed by without some crisis or tension documented in the news. King insisted that the legislature had to pass new and higher taxes before he would give government employees raises.

One bright light came early in the year when the Queen Margrethe II of Denmark and her consort, Prince Heinrich, arrived with their two sons on board their ship of state in March 1976. It was an official visit, and all the red carpets were put out for the lovely thirty–six year old queen whose grandfather had sold the islands to the United States sixty years earlier. Among all the ceremonies, Frits remembers with pride being able to address Her Majesty in Danish

Queen Magrethe II and Prince Heinrich with Frits at Annaly

from the floor of the legislature. Later the Lawaetzes hosted a private party at Annaly for the queen and members of the Friends of Denmark. Frits and Bodil's grandchildren were there and thrilled by it all. They especially liked the two handsome young princes, Fredrik and Joachim. Hans's daughters, Amy and Jodie, watched over Bent's two girls — Simone, age four, and Alice, two and a half years old. The Danes came bearing wonderful gifts which remained on display for months in honor of the bicentennial year.

Another proud moment was the splendid reception given to all visitors during the National Governors' Conference. Islanders

Bodil and Frits Lawaetz, who was named Knight Commander of the Dannebrog by Denmark's Queen Margrethe II

outdid themselves in cleaning up and making St. Croix sparkle for the main event held at Fountain Valley golf course. They even paved the road from Centerline highway to the top of Scenic Drive for smooth access to the golf course. Huge white tents were placed on the greens for the twilight dinner party. It was a beautiful setting and the governors and their spouses loved coming by way of a cruise ship. The meeting did much to improve prospects for St. Croix tourism.

In July 1976, Hess gave an advance of $10 million on the refinery's taxes to ease the financial crisis. He had given $1.25 million in to the government in 1973 for construction of a central St. Croix police facility and had barely been thanked for it. Despite the ill treatment, Leon Hess did care about the islands and went out of his way to assist wherever he could. In June, a special committee had been established to discuss higher taxes for Hess Oil. Frits and Earle Ottley, along with President Elmo Roebuck, were chosen to represent the legislature. Other committee members were Amadeo

Francis, commissioner of commerce; Auguste Rimpel, commissioner of finance; Steve O'Reilly, director of the budget; and Arthur Richards, president of CVI. It was a powerful and knowledgeable group, and they worked in harmony with the men appointed by Leon Hess to negotiate an increased tax rate to help ease the pinch.

Although a second refinery had been approved in 1972 amid intense protest from Crucians, the Twelfth Legislature extended the original agreement for an additional forty months, because the principals could not find investment partners. The original proposers had no refinery experience and were capitalizing on the proximity of Hess Oil to sell their package. Despite the legislature's help, the second refinery never materialized.

While the legislature boiled trying to find ways to stimulate the crashed economy, Cyril King attended every boxing match, funeral, wedding, dinner party and baseball game. And at each one he excoriated the legislature for not giving him *carte blanche* to slap on new taxes. It was tiresome and exhausting for Frits, but it was deadly for the ICM party. King's push for new taxes and his refusal to raise pay led to a ten–week government employee strike and near total losses in the 1976 election. While Democrats were racking up high voter numbers, the lowest being 1,788, only John Bell of St. Croix survived on the ICM ticket with 710 votes. Hector Cintron, an independent candidate, won reelection, and the rest of the seats went to Democrats. It was mass rejection of Cyril King's program. Suddenly King found money in the bank and quickly reversed himself to jockey into position for the election to come in 1978. He, in a frenzy of activity, shelved the demand for new taxes and gave government employees their raises.

By February 1977, Frits was publicly critical of the governor's lack of priorities. He proposed that the two branches get together and work out a plan, instead of just reacting to crises. He noted that funds were removed from an appropriation for the juvenile detention center at Anna's Hope, because it was alleged that federal funds were available; when that proved untrue, too much time was lost before the governor advised the legislature. "We need a master plan for three to five years, not piecemeal appropriations," Frits said. He also spoke about sewage problems because of housing density, insisting that long–range forecasts had to be made "so we can start now to give good service to all these homes on the drawing boards."

Frits was in a fury about the announcement from the Water and Power Authority (WAPA) of the sale of the unfinished south shore power plant, because it was in debt for more than $50 million. Frits went on television in opposition. He said the plant was needed to end constant power outages and to allow excess wattage needed to attract new businesses and industry to St. Croix. He asked how we would power the new industrial parks if WAPA did this and where the new desalinization plant would go. If we had long–term plans in place, the barging of water could be from our own facilities to St. Thomas, instead of from Puerto Rico at top costs. Frits insisted the people of the Virgin Islands deserved no less than a joint agreement, but he was speaking into the wind.

Later on in October, Frits and four of his fellow Crucian senators walked out of a session, protesting the passage of a $26 million bond authorization bill which gave $1 million to build a golf course in St. Thomas, while, as Senator Leroy Arnold said, "Were talking about scrapping to pay employee increases." The session had been called to discuss the budget and employee pay raises due to be passed by 30 September for the start of the new fiscal year; senators had stopped the clock rather than be pressed on the particulars. When various delays were employed, two St. Croix senators, Leroy Arnold and John Bell, walked off the premises in protest. Unfortunately that caused the vote to table the bill to fail, five to six. Then after the Crucian contingent stormed out, Ottley rammed the bill through in a six for, two against, and seven not voting alignment. Senators Roebuck and Cleone Creque Hodge voted no. For Frits it was a return to the days of total control by Earle and "the boys" from St. Thomas. Despite Earle's pledge that St. Croix would get its fair share, Frits wasn't buying it.

— CHAPTER FORTY–TWO —

Juan Luis Becomes Governor

Around the same time in October 1977 as the bond authorization fights, it became known that Cyril King was seriously ill. When the commissioner of health came looking for an appropriation to have Governor King treated for stomach cancer in New York, Senator Ottley told him that authority to take a patient away for treatment unavailable in the territory had already been provided by law. Governor King had vetoed the provision once, but his veto had been overridden and there was no need for an additional authority. The diagnosis was too late for successful treatment; Cyril King died on 2 January 1978, and young Lieutenant Governor Juan Luis stepped into his shoes.

Luis had little previous experience in government. He had been an accountant and was an avid and able baseball player when he first ran for a seat in the Tenth Legislature. His senate service had not been illustrious; he was left in the dust by associates with previous experience, such as Hector Cintron, Claude Molloy and Alex Moorhead. Others he served with were strong personalities: two lawyers named Al Sheen and Brit Bryant, and boisterous Ruby Rouss. During his tenure as lieutenant governor, there had been much friction between Luis and King, for the latter treated him as incidental and did not keep him informed or in the loop of government operations. Yet Luis took hold immediately and vetoed a special pension plan for governors and senators within days of his taking the oath of office. The legislature responded by

Frits's last term in office was with the Twelfth Legislature. Pictured L–R are: Leroy Arnold, Roger Hill, G. Luz A. James, Otis Felix, Eric Dawson, Elmo Roebuck, Cleone Creque Hodge, Britain Bryant, Lloyd Williams, John Bell, Frits Lawaetz, Earle B. Ottley, Sidney Lee, Hector Cintron, John Maduro.

generally keeping a moderate tone for a while, so Governor Luis had time to get a solid grip on the reins of authority.

Frits looked carefully at this new political situation. He was tired of and frustrated with the constant bickering and, lacking the vigor of earlier years, decided he was not willing to begin all over again with a new cabinet. Frits decided to go home and enjoy his family. On the 31 May 1978 Frits announced publicly that this would be his last term.

The 1978 campaign dominated the hearts and minds of the political movers and shakers because Democrats expected to win the governorship. They saw Luis as a novice and a lightweight. DeLugo signed on early to run for the position, choosing Eric Dawson a three–term senator from St. Thomas as his running mate. Dawson had bad marks in St. Croix, because he had once remarked he would much rather have St. Thomas passengers flown through San Juan than give St. Croix's airport an upgrade. That attitude certainly didn't endear him to Frits who had fought for an international airport since the Army had turned Benedict Field over to the territory after the war. Despite that, committed to his party, Frits personally campaigned hard for the DeLugo–Dawson team. So when the Democratic party held a twentieth anniversary testimonial dinner at the Crusaders Club for Frits on his seventy–first birthday and Senator Dawson failed to be there, he lost what few votes he may have been able to salvage from Frits's followers for his arrogance.

The party was a highlight of the campaign on St. Croix. For Frits it was a banner night. In addition to his brothers and their families, all of Frits's sons and their families were present. Despite rainy weather, Senators Johnny Maduro, Roger Hill, Cleone Creque Hodge, Elmo Roebuck and Lloyd Williams were there, as well as the entire legislative contingent from St. Croix and members of the territorial committee. Bodil was presented with a gold necklace and pendant shaped in the number "20," for all her years alone while Frits was in the legislature. Frits himself was presented with a large hand–blown crystal bull, which he immediately pronounced "not a Senepol; this is a Brahma, but I am delighted to have it." The salute lasted well into the night.

Governor Luis, as quickly as he dumped the Democratic party four years previously, now forsook the Independent Citizens Movement and ran as an independent candidate with Henry Millin, a widely respected banker from St. Thomas. Democrats blasted him for lack of loyalties, yet underestimated the motivation of sympathy in people who thought Luis "should be given a chance to show what he could do." The Luis camp ran a tough campaign, with innuendo and blasts at the audacity of white Ron DeLugo trying to go back to old "massa" ways. There was plenty to say about Dawson's alleged anti–St. Croix attitude. When the counting was done, this election was won by the "little guy, the novice" with Luis–Millin getting 12,100 votes compared to 8,111 for DeLugo–Dawson. It was a surprising upset for cocky Democrats who milled around their central party headquarters hour after hour, unable to believe in the midnight results.

— Chapter Forty–Three —

Life as a Senior Statesman

When the new year opened and his retirement began, Frits was not independent of obligations. He served on several blue ribbon commissions and was named chairman by Earle Ottley of the new Ethics and Conflict of Interest Commission. He continued his decades long dedication to the Boy Scouts of America, gave a great deal of time to the Boys Club of which he was a charter member, and was active in the Friends of Denmark. He stayed busy with the St. Croix Association of Handicapped Children and the St. Croix Chamber of Commerce. He had more time now to spend at swim meets, with all four of his granddaughters competing, and was delighted with his first grandson, Frans, born on 10 October 1978 to Sally and Bent. Fritsie and his wife Rachel Speas had a son, Jens, born on 14 August 1979. Rachel and Fritsie lived at first at Annaly mill, but before Jens was born they moved into the manager's house at River, as so many of the Lawaetz family had before them. Rachel liked living at Estate River, but she and Fritsie found they were better friends than marriage partners, so they separated within a year.

Frits was hailed as a senior statesman and was often on call to give speeches and talks to children at schools about life as a senator and as a boy in old Danish times. In 1980 he ran and was elected as a delegate to the Democratic national convention, where Jimmy Carter became the nominee. Frits still finds it amazing that a humble farm boy from little St. Croix could grow up and meet some of the most important men of the United States — in

Congress, the Department of Interior, and the White House. Harry S Truman, thirty–third president, had visited Annaly. Frits met and personally talked with John F. Kennedy, the thirty–fifth president, and Lyndon Baines Johnson, the thirty–sixth, whose inauguration he attended. He also attended the swearing in of James Earl Carter of Georgia, the thirty–ninth president, and met him many times thereafter. In 1988 he would greet one more: Republican nominee George Bush, soon to become the forty–first president, came on a brief swing through the territory and was feted at Government House St. Croix.

In 1980, the Democrats went back once more to Frits for help, this time to ask him to encourage one of his sons to run for the legislature. They wanted a Lawaetz back in office. Frits said he would talk to the family. After much discussion Bent agreed to run, campaigned hard and placed very well in the elections. Differing in style from Frits, but equally as effective, Bent served his district well for ten of the next twelve years, and he held the office of president of the legislature for one of those terms.

With Bent as a member, Frits followed quite closely the proceedings of the Fourth Constitutional Convention in 1981. During this convention the acrimonious debate about whether a Virgin Islander born abroad would be eligible to run for the governorship split the population on the issue of special privilege. Identifying a point in time for one to be truly a "Virgin Islander" or "native born" has remained a debating point up to present time.

Most debaters on the street and in the convention were not aware of the historic record showing that many nineteenth century native–born or creole islanders had quickly abandoned St. Croix in the early days following the 1848 emancipation. A new wave of people came in from the British, French and Dutch isles during the second half of the nineteenth century; many of their children took to their heels during the dismal doldrums of the 1920s. Residents whose roots went back generations, including the Lawaetzes, were very much in the minority by the early 1970s, as immigration from both the US and the other Caribbean islands swelled the territory's population to 96,000. Defining which wave of "native sons" qualified caused bitter fights and has thwarted the creation of a constitution for Virgin Islanders by Virgin Islanders to the present day.

Fritsie and son Jens, circa 1984

Above, Frits with most of his grandchildren, circa 1987. Back (l–r): Simone, Amy, Alice. Front (l–r): Frans, Frits, Jens.

At left, Bent Lawaetz, sworn in as president of the Legislature of the Virgin Islands, January 1989.

— Chapter Forty–Four —

An Estate History

Ward Canaday died quite unexpectedly of a heart attack on 27 February 1976. His will gave title to the registrations and trade marks on the Senepol cattle to the partnership shareholders, Frits, Hans and Fritsie, and gave his properties to his daughter and grandchildren. Ward Canaday had just one daughter, Doreen, whose husband was a professor at Princeton. All three Lawaetz partners paid their last respects to Frits's boss and partner of thirty–six years by attending Ward Canaday's Toledo funeral, although for them it was frigid weather.

In the ensuing years Doreen decided that neither she nor her heirs had a personal interest in maintaining a stake in the cattle business or in holding her father's remaining properties in St. Croix. They eventually decided to sell the property. In 1982, the Annaly Farms partnership agreed to buy the Annaly homestead from the Canaday heirs. The purchase of thirty–four acres included the mill, factory ruins and the main house where Bodil and Frits had lived for forty–three years. The purchase was completed in 1983. Frits remembers it was a proud day to stand on the stairs at Annaly with Bodil and know the farm, as far as the eye could see, belonged to them all. Doreen's grandchildren do return as friends and spend time with the Lawaetzes, strengthening bonds built through the twentieth century.

When Frits bought Annaly, he inherited all of its papers.

Annaly was first developed as a plantation in the eighteenth century by Nicholas Tuite, an Irish planter from Montserrat and a devout Catholic. The Danish West India Company purchased St. Croix in 1733, and, in order to lure experienced farmers to the island, Denmark's king granted a special dispensation to Catholics that allowed them to openly support their own religion. Tuite had visited Governor General Jens Hansen in 1749 and was promised religious tolerance and given official permission to bring in his own Capuchin monk. Once Hansen's permission was made official by the king in 1754, Tuite moved to St. Croix with dozens of families, adding more than a thousand whites and blacks to the population. He acquired lots seventeen and eighteen of Northside A, named them Estate Annaly and erected his residence and a chapel there by 1767.

In 1786, the property went to Roger Ferrals (also spelled Ferrall, Ferrells, etc.), another planter from the British island of Montserrat. For a while during the Ferrall years the estate was owned partly by two house slaves during their lifetime, an unusual gift. By 1794 a windmill was erected. It may have suffered blows from a hurricane, as the standing mill carries the date of 1803. Frits found notes indicating that, in 1816, Annaly had 194 slaves and 318 acres in pasture, 220 in sugar canes. It was one of the few plantations capable of producing 250,000 net pounds of sugar annually.

Annaly at one point was comprised of the estates Rose Hill, Spring Garden, Caledonia, Nicholas and Mt. Victory, more than 1,100 acres. The estate stayed in Farrell family hands until 1855; Quintin Dick owned it through 1862. In the early 1860s, a steam mill imported from Scotland produced 300,000 net pounds of sugar for the mega–estate. It was owned by a W. Plaskett until 1876, when William Moore took ownership.

Eighteen seventy–six was a time of drought and severe deprivation. Workers were under harsh rules of labor, unable to leave the island or change jobs except once a year — October first. On 1 October 1878 a labor insurrection began in Frederiksted. Known as "Fireburn," it was a major workers' uprising. Workers demanded fair pay equal to government central factory workers and changes in labor contract laws, among other things. Rumors were running that a town drunk had been beaten and killed, and the mob charged to the hospital to find the truth. However, the doctor and police master fled to Fort Frederik, just a few blocks down the waterfront street, before the mob arrived at the hospital. Moving to the fort the group demanded answers. Receiving none, they began throwing stones and conch shells, and, in turn, the police master ordered his troops to open fire. It was after noon of the next day when the message of rioting reached the vice–governor in Christiansted, who sent a small troop of soldiers to quell the disturbance. Frederiksted stores, including Moore's, were ransacked through the night of 1 October. The mob also burnt down Moore's store and his home above it. William Moore was specifically named as inciting the gathered workers with his harsh words. He was then chased from his Frederiksted townhouse by a mob and forced to hide the night through in waist–deep water under the town wharf. In the four major days of unrest, Estate Annaly's greathouse and factory, owned by Moore, were burned to the ground. Nearly fifty plantations were in ruins and more than a hundred people died. After Moore died of pneumonia a month later, it was learned that he was bankrupt.

Mr. Hallensen bought Annaly at auction in December 1879 and rebuilt the factory and greathouse. During Hallensen's ownership, the school house parcel, which is quite close to the estate house, was separated from the estate and set aside.

Between February 1902 until Canaday's purchase in November 1936, Annaly belonged to Andrew J. Blackwood, a sea captain on ships sailing between New York and St. Croix. He also was a spokesman and factor for Bartram Brothers Company and, at one time, was owner of Golden Grove, a property which later became the core of the St. Croix campus of the College of the Virgin Islands. Blackwood was the grandfather and guardian of Frits's boyhood friend and competitor for first honors in grammar school, Ralph Skeoch.

Annaly's greathouse, listed in the National Register of Historic Places in January 1979, is noted in particular for its triple arch, for its heavy molding in the reception room and for the fine nineteenth century cast–iron rim locks and butts on interior doors. The house is a classic West Indian home, with a central set of rooms — entry, reception and gallery — flanked by matching large airy bedrooms to the east and west ends. It has a massive attic with high ceilings under hip roof, and below are a series of cellars large enough to house whole families in times of bad weather, which it has done many times.

Bodil reclaimed this house from the neglect of years, and it is today a place of great charm with West Indian tables and chairs, as well as a few more modern couches. Frits and Bodil kept their desks in the original entry hall, which was seldom used to enter the house, as they preferred to use the terrace door on the north side. The attached kitchen still has its original 1879 raised fireplace now inset with a modern cooktop.

Near the back kitchen door stands Bodil's equipment from the National Weather Service which she operated daily beginning in 1957.

When the monster hurricane, Hugo, hit on 17–18 September 1989, raging at more than two hundred miles an hour, the Lawaetzes had some of their neighbors with them down in the cellars at Annaly. Hugo tore off the main house roof, sparing only the kitchen area. Young cowboys later installed canvas tarps over the living room, and for a while Frits and Bodil managed to live in the kitchen before moving into the mill house with Fritsie around December of that year. Later they moved to St. Croix by the Sea Hotel, owned by brother Erik and Jenny. They enjoyed being there and playing poker at night. Usually they bet pennies, but once a little pig was wagered. Another time, a chair was placed in the poker pot. It was fun, but they really wanted to go home.

Annaly wasn't ready until the 31 April 1991, because the Annaly Farm workers first repaired the St. Croix by the Sea Hotel, in order to house construction workers for the island. Then they repaired the family's private homes. The Lawaetz family had the hard job of deciding whether or not to rebuild Annaly, because of the great expense involved. Eventually the partners voted to apply for a large loan and restore it to its original style.

Bent, when home from boarding school, helped Miss Clarke with charcoal cooking in the Annaly kitchen.

— Chapter Forty–Five —

A Lifetime of Memories

The 1980s and 1990s were filled with memorable occasions for Frits. On 4 February 1984 Frits and Alva McFarlane were jointly given the first Distinguished Citizen Awards by the Virgin Islands Council, Boy Scouts of America. Frits specifically was recognized for his involvement with the council since 1950. The tall bronze replica of the "ideal Boy Scout" sculpture holds the premier spot on the Lawaetz center table at Annaly. Frits also received the St. Croix Chamber of Commerce's 1985 Humanitarian Award. He was specifically chosen because it was International Youth Year, and the award was given out of deep respect for "his total commitment to the interests, growth and development of our island youth." There were many recognitions and honors, but those two stand out as very precious memories to Frits. He also is proud of another, this from his government, which by legislation enacted in 1982, named the Lagoon Street Homes in Frederiksted the "Frits Eduard Lawaetz Homes." Its dedication did not come until 6 October 1994, but was nonetheless just as sweet.

In the 1980s, Bodil was recognized also for her continuous efforts on behalf of the USO. In September 1987 she was also honored by the U.S. Department of Commerce as one of just twenty–five recipients of the highest honor in the National Weather Service, the John Campanius Holm Award. She was chosen from a field of more than twelve thousand keepers of records across the

In 1982, Lagoon Street homes were named for Frits, in honor "of his many years of dedicated service to the people of the Virgin Islands." The dedication, pictured above, took place in 1994. Bodil and Frits are on the left.

country, and the men in her family were bursting with pride for her recognition.

Life seemed particularly grand: they had watched with pride when Jodie, their second eldest granddaughter and a champion swimmer, was honored to carry the Virgin Islands flag in the parade of athletes at the 1984 Olympic Games in Los Angeles. When the television feed placed an ad right during the V.I. entry march, Frits for once used his connections, and Laurence Rockefeller was able to get an unedited copy of the parade for Frits and the family.

In 1985 Bodil and Frits gave a grand party to celebrate their fiftieth wedding anniversary, inviting more than four hundred guests, including all of his old legislative employees, Toby Schoyer, Cherra Heyliger, Miriam Powell's family, Cheo Guadeloupe, Gus Doward, Leroy Arnold, and Joy James, as well as his often summer intern, Violet Anne Golden, namesake of his childhood friend, Violet Pedersen of Ham's Bluff. Frits says there were others he can't recall now, but the party was wall–to–wall well wishers, with few dry eyes when Frits danced the anniversary waltz with his beautiful bride. Later Frits read a little poem he had written for Bodil.

In December 1987, Frits got another taste of mortality when, during cattle weighing time, he was crushed against his car by two bulls fighting. His recovery required time in the hospital and another month in bed. Fritsie and Hans were adamant that the eighty–year old cowboy give up the physical work and stick to the paper work!

Young Fritsie was by now very active in the Democratic party, an elected territorial committee member. He was nominated to the Virgin Islands Board of Parole in 1989 which made Frits very proud. Fritsie eventually became chairman of the board of parole.

Fritsie became ill late in 1989. The initial diagnosis was possibly cancer, but it wasn't that. He recovered and resumed his duties. Early in 1990 Fritsie separated from his second wife, Lillie, whom he had married in 1986, and moved into the mill house at Annaly. After Frits and Bodil returned to the main house in 1991, they were happy to have Jens nearby when he came for his weekend visits with his father.

Frits and Bodil went to Denmark in 1992. Frits was the American keynote speaker at the Fourth of July celebration of U.S. independence at Rebild, Denmark, a very special honor. He and Bodil had a wonderful time with family and friends.

In 1994 they returned to Denmark with the Friends of Denmark and helped their close friends, Bent and Hannah Rasmussen of the Top Hat Restaurant in Christiansted, celebrate their silver wedding anniversary there. Then they moved on to England, so Bodil and her twin Annette could jointly celebrate their eighty–fifth birthdays on 23 July. The party was held at Graham and Annette's home in Bristol with all the European relatives present, as well as Fritsie, his son Jens, and Fritsie's close companion, Mary Roebuck, from St. Croix.

During this trip Frits and Fritsie noticed that Bodil was having trouble remembering people, both those she knew well in Denmark, and the younger generations. They were particularly concerned when she had trouble recalling her own sister and couldn't always say the right word, whether in English or Danish. Time would prove this to be an unfortunate but natural hazard of aging, in Bodil's case, probably Alzheimer's disease.

The Bull and his helpers at Annaly: Alfonzo "Wyson" Correa on Thor; standing (l–r) Fritsie, Frits, Augustin Bermudez, Benjamin Ramos, Ralph George; kneeling (l–r) Jonathon Hitesman, Tonio Bermudez, Jose Carlos Ponce.

The following year, Frits's sister Else, eighty–eight, died in Denmark on 25 August 1993. Her long held wish was to have her ashes returned to Little La Grange which she loved so much. Her children and grandchildren concurred. Anna, age eighty–nine, who had long been in the care of Irene and Kai, died not long after on 21 October, and a joint interring of ashes was held for the two sisters at the family gravesite at Little La Grange.

Bodil's health began to deteriorate along with her memory. The next years became a struggle. Yet, it never occurred to Frits to do other than what he did: he took care of Bodil, as she had taken care of him for so many years. He helped her dress, combed her hair, coaxed her into eating, and took her for drives through the green hillsides around Annaly Farms and down to the post office in Frederiksted every day.

Complicating emotions during these years was the fact that Fritsie's health problems did not respond to treatment. Most of the time he was well, but at times totally exhausted. Fritsie was serving as chairman of the parole board when he died on 17 March 1996 at the age of forty–six. Mary and Jens were by his side. The funeral was private; Fritsie was buried at Little La Grange, by the graves of his grandparents. Life slowly resumed normalcy, as time marched on toward the new century.

For some time, the elder Lawaetzes had been discussing the long–term future of the family home at Little La Grange. Frits and Erik had received parcels of land from their mother in the 1950s. When Mor died in 1964, Kai was given a similar amount of land at #7 Little La Grange, and all of her five surviving children jointly inherited the Little La Grange homestead and nineteen acres of surrounding lands, as well as #7 Jolly Hill. The brothers knew from island experience that leaving the disposition of this legacy to multiple third–generation heirs would complicate family relations. Disposition had been somewhat settled in 1989 during a visit home by Else, when the sisters had released their claims on the homestead for lifetime rights and the proceeds from the sale of #7 Jolly Hill.

After hurricane Hugo damaged the house, Kai and Irene built a new home for themselves high on the hill by the old mill. A decision had to be made about who would take on the responsibility of managing the family home. After exploratory discussions with the St. Croix Landmarks Society, a local historic preservation organization formerly called the St. Croix Landmarks League, the family formed a corporation and signed a long–term agreement with the society. (Both Frits and Jenny had been members of the board of trustees at various times.) The society would be responsible for managing the house and nineteen acres as a museum in

In 1996 the family dedicated Little La Grange as a museum honoring Carl and Marie.

Front row (l–r) kneeling: Irene (Kai's wife), Carly Kauffman (Kai's granddaughter), Amy Howell (Hans's daughter), Frans (Bent's son), Bent, Jens (Fritsie's son), Rory Kauffman (Kai's grandson).

Second row (l–r): Jodie Mays (Hans's daughter), Judy (Hans's wife), Susanne Kauffman (Kai's daughter), Sally (Bent's wife), Bodil and Frits.

Third row (l–r): Hans holding grandson Bryson Mays, Brent Mays (Hans's son–in–law) holding Tyler Howell, Aden Kauffman [wearing hat] (Kai's son–in–law), David (Erik's son), Kai, Jenny (Erik's wife), Erik, and Mona (Erik's daughter).

honor of Carl and Marie. Arrangements were concluded in 1996, one hundred years after Carl bought the property, sight unseen.

Irene Lawaetz was retained as manager to give tours as she has gracefully done for so many visitors from Denmark since her marriage to Kai in 1956. Special days were reserved for family events: Christmas Eve, Christmas day and New Year's day will be celebrated there for as long as the family wishes. Carl and Marie's joint birthday, 7 March, and a celebration of Transfer Day will continue to be held there as well. Respect for the past and its traditions are ties that keep a family together, Frits believes. The past must be remembered, he thinks, to better prepare for the future.

The same year that his childhood home became a museum, Frits began to get his papers together for this biography. He continued to give advice to politicians and would–be politicians. He continued to dress, feed and then walk with Bodil as she chose. She suffered, and he suffered, through the course of the physical decay until she slipped quietly away on Sunday morning, 3 October 1999 with Frits holding her hand. Her ashes were placed near those of her son Fritsie and the rest of the family in the garden at Little La Grange.

The new century, Frits says, will be very different. Annaly Farms now can only get one–year leases on its two thousand rented acres. This means no more five–year plans, because the land can be sold away and the rental rights abrogated with a month's notice. Yet Annaly Farms partnership and Senepol cattle will survive through the stock now growing in twenty–two states and many foreign countries; there are Senepol breeders worldwide to carry on. Frits also feels that unless the territory gets back on track and educates its people for the job market with apprenticeship programs, strangers will continue to come in and take the skilled jobs. But Frits sees potentials too: his granddaughter Jodie left her real estate career after hurricane Hugo hit in 1989 and took over the management of the meat market operation, so her father, Hans, could direct their recovery efforts. Bent's two daughters have completed university, and, as of 2000, his son Frans has graduated and is working in Boston. Young Jens was coached by Frits through his preparatory school through constant letters and telephone calls. Jens is not preparing for cattle ranching, which he does not choose (at least not yet). Instead, considering a career at sea, he started at the Maritime Academy in Maine in the fall of 1999.

Frits keeps in touch with grassroots political efforts here in the territory and with the Atlanta Project founded by Jimmy and Rosalynn Carter, of which Frits is a financial supporter. He talks to school classes as an expert in the "ancient history" of his childhood and attends and often speaks at occasions of state such as Emancipation Day, Transfer Day and the Hurricane Supplication Days. He finds that too often he is attending funerals of friends and allies much younger than himself, but that is one side of living ably past the age of ninety–three and counting. And he gives generously of his time to aspiring politicians, to students of history, to reporters and others who wonder what it must be like to be more than ninety and who want to hear about the vast changes Frits has seen in his birthplace, St. Croix. His conviction remains that it was and is his duty to serve his country and, by hard work, to make it a little better than it was before he tried.

Frits with great grandson Bryson.

The Hans Lawaetz family about 1996 (L–R): Steve Howell holding Tyler Howell, Amy Howell, Hans Lawaetz holding Bryson Mays, Judy Lawaetz, Jodie Mays and Brent Mays

Honors and Awards

Frits has received many awards and salutations during his lifetime. Those that touched him most recognized his work with youngsters and his work on behalf of the people of St. Croix when he served on the St. Croix Soil and Water Conservation District Board and in the Virgin Islands Legislature.

1969 American Methodist Episcopal Church, for his work in general

1972 For his training of soldiers as captain in the Home Guard

1972 V.I. Department of Agriculture for valuable service

1976 Knight Commander of the Dannebrog from Her Majesty Queen Magrethe of Denmark

1978 Democratic Party testimonial as "Man of Service to the People"

1978 Resolution 964, the Legislature of the Virgin Islands, to honor Senator Frits E. Lawaetz (See text following.)

1982 Lagoon Street Complex is named in his honor; dedicated in 1994

1984 Boy Scouts of America, V.I. Council, Distinguished Citizen Award

1985 St. Croix Chamber of Commerce, Humanitarian Award

1986 Frederiksted Friendship Basket Ball League

1987 Boys Clubs of America, Certificate for Outstanding Public Service

1990 Holy Trinity Lutheran Church, Frederiksted, Outstanding Service Certificate

1991 Boy Scouts of America, V.I. Council, for long–term executive board service

1993 Georgia Senepol Association honors

1994 American keynote speaker at Fourth of July celebration in Rebild, Denmark

2000 V.I. Department of Agriculture, Cattleman of the Twentieth Century

2000 Boy Scouts of America, V.I. Council, James E. West Award

Resolution No. 964

Bill No. 8085

Twelfth Legislature of the Virgin Islands of the United States

Regular Session

1978

To honor Senator Frits E. Lawaetz

— *o* —

Whereas in *Profiles in Courage* John F. Kennedy wrote: "A democracy that has...no monument of individual conscience in a sea of popular rule—is not worthy to bear the name. The true democracy, living and growing and inspiring, puts its faith in the people — faith that the people will not simply elect men who will represent their views ably and faithfully, but also elect men of conscientious judgment – faith that the people will not condemn those whose devotion to principle leads them to unpopular courses, but will reward courage, respect honor and ultimately recognize right;" and

Whereas the United States Virgin Islands has been graced with such a monument of individual conscience in Senator Frits Lawaetz, a man who has served his people with this conscientious judgment and devotion to principle; and

WHEREAS the Lawaetz name has been a part of the fabric of Virgin Islands history for more than a century; and

WHEREAS born the son of Carl and Marie Lawaetz on October 5, 1907, at Estate Little La Grange, Danish West Indies, Frits Lawaetz has lived and worked in the Frederiksted area for 71 years; and

WHEREAS he is so much a part of his native land that he is affectionately and widely known as the "Bull of Annaly" and the "Senator from Annaly;" and

WHEREAS Frits Lawaetz has been a participant in and a keen observer and recorder of many decades of the history of the Islands; and

WHEREAS through his writings, speeches and conversations, countless Virgin Islanders, especially the youth, have gained knowledge and insight into the years of Danish rule, purchase and transfer of the Islands to the United States, and the development of agriculture and the sugar cane industry; and

WHEREAS he has sought to preserve the Danish heritage through his knowledge of the Danish language, translation of documents, contacts with the Danish people both here and in Denmark, and as member and President of the Friends of Denmark Society; and

WHEREAS Frits Lawaetz has been active in efforts to restore and preserve historical sites in the Virgin Islands; and

WHEREAS trained in agriculture science in Denmark, Frits Lawaetz is a longtime farmer and rancher who has tested and developed new methods in soil conservation, water retention, and the raising of cattle, grain and sugar cane; and

WHEREAS in his public life, Frits Lawaetz has been an outspoken supporter of the Virgin Islands farmer and has devoted considerable time and effort to the development of Virgin Islands agriculture; and

WHEREAS as an ardent sports fan he has given moral and financial support to all forms of athletics, is a vigorous supporter of Virgin Islands teams and athletes participating in inter–island and inter–American contests, has bred and raised racing horses, and has sponsored and supported legislation to construct and improve sporting facilities; and

WHEREAS on November 2, 1954, Frits Lawaetz received more votes than any other candidate to represent the District of St. Croix in the First Legislature of the Virgin Islands; and

WHEREAS with the exception of four years, he has been a member of the Virgin Islands Legislature since its creation and in this position has been a powerful and guiding force in the development of the modern Virgin Islands; and

WHEREAS during times of political dissension and bitterness, Frits Lawaetz was a moderating voice; and

WHEREAS as a leader of the "Donkey" wing of the Democratic Party, he was instrumental in its unification with the "Mortar and Pestle" group into what is now the Democratic Party; and

WHEREAS a measure of the popularity and respect enjoyed by Frits Lawaetz can be seen in headlines and descriptive phrases of the man found in the popular press throughout his long career: "A man of little talk but much action." "One of the most honorable men in the Virgin Islands Legislature." "The veracity and integrity...we have heard no one question." And

WHEREAS the love felt by the people of the Virgin

Islands for Frits Lawaetz is perhaps best demonstrated by the headline over an article in the *Westend News* in announcing that the Senator continued to improve following a serious operation on the mainland. The headline stated simply: "St. Croix Overjoyed." Now, Therefore,

Be it resolved by the Legislature of the Virgin Islands:

Section 1. On behalf of all the people of the Virgin Islands, the Legislature hereby honors Senator Frits Lawaetz and thanks him for his long and outstanding service to these islands. He is among the finest statesmen to come forward to do the people's business.

Section 2. A perma plaque copy of this Resolution shall be prepared and presented to Senator Frits Lawaetz by the President of the Legislature at a special ceremony held for that purpose.

Thus passed by the Legislature of the Virgin Islands on October 12, 1978.

Witness our Hands and the Seal of the Legislature of the Virgin Islands this 12th Day of October, A.D. 1978.

/signed/ Elmo D. Roebuck
Elmo D. Roebuck
President

/signed/ Eric E. Dawson
Eric E. Dawson
Legislative Secretary

Glossary

andagt – small religious devotion or prayers said for a special purpose

apothecary – dispensary of drugs and medications, government sanctioned in Danish times

auction – public competitive bidding sale of property, usually to pay debts, at times because of planned permanent departure of the owner

baby book – a book of photos and handwritten notes about a child's life

britches – from "breech" material for the lower torso, gathered to cross and breech between legs; knee–length pants

cay – pronounced "key," a small island; some may be inhabited

cart – small open vehicle usually with seating for one person, space for materials, often made with just two wheels, pulled by a horse, donkey or even a goat

central factory – a cooperative processing plant for pressing juices from sugar canes

chiggers – larvae of a parasitic mite that causes much itching

Christiansted – one of two major towns in St. Croix, on northeast portion of the island

cistern – an enclosed masonry tank used to hold rain water captured from roofs

cookhouse – an independent building for cooking meals and heating water

crown properties – the king of Denmark and his family had property investments managed by the government

Dane – a citizen of Denmark, a 10,000 year old kingdom in northern Europe

Danish West Indies – located in the Caribbean Sea approximately

18 degrees north, 64 west, made of St. Croix, St. John, St. Thomas and forty other cays

Dannebrog – Danish flag

deaconess – a Luthern church ministry of sisters dedicated to social service work

dengue fever – a tropical infection with severe joint and muscle pains, also called breakbone

elephantiasis – painful swelling of a limb caused by worms

estate – in the Danish West Indies, estates had been set at roughly 150 Danish acres, each considered sufficient for a plantation in 1733, where one grew crops or raised livestock

far – Danish name for father

farfar – Danish name for paternal grandfather

farmor – Danish name for paternal grandmother

gaard – Danish word for farm, as in Raefsnaesgaard, farm of or at Raefsnaes

Great War – World War I, 1914–1918

gut – a water course for springs or intermittent streams after rainfall

heifer – a grown female cattle that has not yet borne a calf

Jumbie Bush – an area of La Grange to the east of the cemetery in Frederiksted, many trees

malaria – a parasitic infection carried by mosquitos, producing chills, fever, sweating, aches

mongoose – four–legged animal, similar in looks to a squirrel but not as fast

mor – Danish name for mother

morfar – Danish name for maternal grandfather

mormor – Danish name for maternal grandmother

N'Dama – cattle from Senegal, West Africa, gentle, hardy, tsetse–fly resistant

oberst loejnant – senior lieutenant in Danish militia

outhouse – an enclosed toilet facility apart from the main house

plantation – another name for "estate," which included village housing for workers

provisions ground – plot of land given over to raising vegetables and herbs for the family's consumption.

provisions – word given to home–grown vegetables. Often such gardens were devoted entirely to root vegetables — peanuts, potatoes, yam, cassava

puttekammer – a room Carl built, which was used for general storage and photo printing

reservoir – place where anything is collected and stored, generally in large quantities. Can be a natural or artificial lake or pond, sometimes created by an earthen dam, in which water is collected and stored for use.

sted – on the end of a name is Danish word for town, i.e., Christiansted = Christian's town

stevedores – cargo handlers for goods going to or from a ship

titty bread – a small loaf with pointed ends, roughly eight to ten inches long

vortice – pattern of hair growth in a circular motion

Bibliography

Canegata, D.C. *St. Croix at the 20th Century: A Chapter in its History.* New York: Carlton Press, Inc., c. 1968.

Carruth, Gordon. *What Happened When.* 1991 edition. North Carolina: Signet, c. 1989.

College of the Virgin Islands. Report 11. *Senepol Cattle: History and Development.* St. Croix, Virgin Islands: Agricultural Experiment Station, CVI St. Croix, Second (Revised) Printing July 1981.

Dept. of Education. *An Historical Account of the Purchase and Transfer of the DWI.* St. Croix V.I., March 14, 1969.

Dept. of Planning and Natural Resources, Div. of Libraries, Archives and Museums. *Blue Book.* 1991–1992. USVI, Fourth Edition.

Dookhan, Isaac. *A History of the Virgin Islands of the United States.* Jamaica: Canoe Press, c. 1994.

Hansen, Axel C. *From These Shores.* Nashville, Tennessee: JM Publications, c. 1996.

Jacobsen, Helge Seidelin. *An Outline History of Denmark.* Copenhagen: Host & Son, 1986.

Lawaetz, Erik J. *St. Croix: 500 Years: Pre Columbus to 1990.* Copenhagen: Poul Kristensen, 1991.

Lawaetz, Marie Nyeborg. Frits Eduard Lawaetz Baby Book, 1907–1922. Private papers of Frits E. Lawaetz.

Lewisohn, Florence. *St. Croix Under Seven Flags.* Florida: Dukane Press, c. 1970.

Nuland, Sherwin B. *How We Die.* New York: Random House, c. 1993.

Ottley, Earle B. *Trials and Triumphs.* Charlotte Amalie, St. Thomas V.I., c. 1982.

Senepol Cattle Breeders Association. *Senepol World.* Kansas City, Missouri, Summer 1997.

Poole, Bernard L. *The Caribbean Commission.* Columbia, South Carolina: University of South Carolina Press, c. 1951.

Rouse, John. E. *World Cattle.* Vol. 3, "Cattle of North America." Norman, Oklahoma: University of Oklahoma, c. 1973.

Steif, William. "Hybrids for High Performance." *Americas* 48:1 (1996): 4.

Steif, William. "Caribbean Cattle" *U.S./Latin Trade* (December 1994): 26.

Taylor, Charles Edwin. Leaflets of the Danish West Indies. St. Thomas V.I.

Tucker, Rufus S. *Economic Conditions of the Virgin Islands.* Document #110. 69th Congress, 1st Session of the U.S. Senate, 1926.

Willocks, Harold W. *The Umbilical Cord: the History of the United States Virgin Islands from Pre–Columbian Era to the Present.* Christiansted, St. Croix, V.I., c. 1995.

• • •

A large amount of materials came from private collections, many of which were undated. Periodicals included:

Berlingske Tidende, Copenhagen, Bagsiden article of 2 July 1992.

Bien. Weekly Danish Newspaper, Los Angeles, CA 90046

Daily News of the Virgin Islands.

Der Danske Pioneer. Hoffman Estates, Illinois: Bertelsen Publishing Co., Marts 16, 1992

Jyllands Posten. Copenhagen. "Morgennavisen." 29 March 1992

Legislative Record of the First Legislature, April 9–June 6, 1957 and April 14–June 12, 1958.

The Home Journal. St. Thomas V.I.

St. Croix Avis. St. Croix, V.I.

Senepol. Senepol Cattle Breeders Association. Kansas City, Mo.

Session Laws of the Virgin Islands.

Virgin Islands Times. St. Croix.

The West End News. Frederiksted, St. Croix.

Three organizations were also of great help: (1) Annaly Farms Inc. for its Senepol History 1931–1991, a three–ring binder of historical documents and photos showing involvement with Senegal, Red Poll and the resultant Senepol breed; (2) the Virgin Islands public libraries in Charlotte Amalie, Christiansted and Frederiksted; and (3) the research library at Whim Plantation Museum, St. Croix, where there are many unpublished, typed manuscripts produced by Eva Lawaetz, cousin of Frits Lawaetz and an employee for many years of the archival division of the Virgin Islands government. Eva researched and translated documents in the Danish archives pertinent to the Virgin Islands on a large variety of topics which may be found in the vertical files. Material also was gleaned from census data gathered by the Danish government and the United States of America, available on microfilm in the research library at Whim Plantation Museum, St. Croix.

Index

A

B

F

I

T

W

Y

Z

About the Author

Priscilla Galvin Watkins honed her political skills working with Democratic members of the Legislature of the Virgin Islands as an analyst over two decades before moving to the executive branch for eight years. Interest in history led to authorship of several publications of local interest, *For the Country People* (1975), *Government House St. Croix* (1996), and *Preserving the Legacy* (1998). A friend and admirer of Frits Lawaetz, this is her first biography.